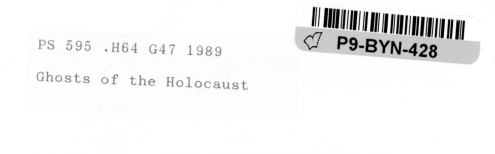

GHOSTS OF THE
HOLOCAUST

GHOSTS OF THE HOLOCAUST

*An Anthology
of Poetry
by the
Second Generation*

Edited by Stewart J. Florsheim
Foreword by Gerald Stern

Wayne State University Press
Detroit
1989

Library of Congress Cataloging-in-Publication Data

Ghosts of the Holocaust : an anthology of poetry by the
   second generation / edited by Stewart J. Florsheim ;
   foreword by Gerald Stern.
         p.   cm.
      Includes index.
      ISBN 0–8143–2052–X (alk. paper)
      1. Holocaust, Jewish (1939–1945)—Poetry. 2. Jews—
Poetry. 3. War victims—Poetry. 4. Concentration camps
—Poetry. 5. World War, 1939–1945—Poetry.
6. American poetry—Jewish authors. 7. American poetry
—20th century. 8. English poetry—Jewish authors.
9. English poetry—20th century. 10. Children of
Holocaust survivors, Writings of.   I. Florsheim,
Stewart J., 1952–

PS595 H64G47 1989
811'.54'0808924—dc19   88–18576
                                                CIP

Marvin Bell, "The Extermination of the Jews" from
A Probable Volume of Dreams. Copyright © 1969 Marvin
Bell. Reprinted with the permission of Atheneum
Publishers, an imprint of Macmillan Publishing Co.

Marvin Bell, "Getting Lost in Nazi Germany" from *The
Escape into You.* Copyright © 1971 Marvin Bell.
Reprinted with the permission of Atheneum Publishers,
an imprint of Macmillan Publishing Co.

To my parents, who fled Germany; my grandfather, who survived Dachau; and my family, who perished in the camps: you inspired my life with the meaning of survival.

Mark the first page of the book with a red marker.
For, in the beginning, the wound is invisible.

—Edmond Jabés
The Book of Questions

Contents

Foreword *by Gerald Stern*   15

Preface   19

I.   ASSEMBLING THE DEAD

    Stephen Berg
      Desnos Reading the Palms of Men on Their Way to
      the Gas Chambers   23

    Stewart J. Florsheim
      Real Chocolate   30

    William Heyen
      Blue   32

    William Heyen
      The Trains   34

    Barbara Helfgott Hyett
      Assembling the Dead at Dachau   35

    Lyn Lifshin
      Crystal Night   36

    Lyn Lifshin
      Seeing the Documentary by the British Liberating
      Bergen-Belsen   38

    Lyn Lifshin
      Bergen-Belsen 1945   39

    Richard Michelson
      Interrogation   40

    Richard Michelson
      Faraway Landscape   41

    Anne Ranasinghe
      Holocaust 1944   42

    Enid Shomer
      Women Bathing at Bergen-Belsen   44

II.   FAMILY ALBUM

    Karen Alkalay-Gut
      Life Goes on   47

    Annette Bialik Harchik
      Requiem   48

Contents

William Heyen
For Hermann Heyen 50
Phyllis Kahaney
Pogrom 51
Sharon Kessler
Family Secrets 52
Sharon Kessler
Names the Dead Speak 53
Denyse Kirsch
Dvora 54
Steven C. Levi
Abbienti 55
Seymour Mayne
Zalman 57
Mark Nepo
The Oil of Her Hands 58
Amos Neufeld
Family Album 59
Amos Neufeld
Pictures and Stories 60
Evelyn Posamentier
Being Modern in Jerusalem 61
Evelyn Posamentier
The Hungarian Medical Student: 1928 63
Lisa Ress
The Family Album 65
Marie Syrkin
My Uncle in Treblinka 66
Evelyn Wexler
The Governess 67
Merra Young-Prottengeier
Lithuanian Grandmother 69

III. FAR FROM AUSCHWITZ

BonniLee
White Candles 73
Cheryl J. Fish
Work and Worry 76
Stewart J. Florsheim
Weekend in Palm Springs 78
Barbara Goldberg
Survivor 80
Annette Bialik Harchik
Earrings 82

Contents

Lyn Lifshin
I Remember Haifa Being Lovely But   83
Gail Newman
Photograph of Survivors   84
Gary Pacernick
Louie the Tailor   85
Lisa Ress
Waving Her Farewell. Train Station, Vienna XV, 1939   86
Elizabeth Rosner
Souvenirs   87
Barry Sternlieb
Survivor   88
Morrie Warshawski
Sonia at 32   89
Florence Weinberger
Survivor   90
Florence Weinberger
He Wears Old Socks   91
Will Wells
Beatings   92

IV. I AM YOUR AMERICAN CHILD

Joan (Thaler) Dobbie
Forty Three Years After Hitler My
Parents Visit Eugene   95
Stewart J. Florsheim
The Jewish Singles Event   97
Stewart J. Florsheim
Business in Germany   99
Florence Wallach Freed
A Private School for Girls
May 14, 1948, New York City   102
Sari Friedman
Answering Machine Message   103
Sari Friedman
Skin   104
Barbara Goldberg
Our Father   107
Richard Michelson
The Queen Esther Award   108
Richard Michelson
The Jews That We Are   110
Richard Michelson
Where I Sat   112

Contents

Gail Newman
Recording History   114
Evelyn Posamentier
Counting Backwards   115
Evelyn Posamentier
The Bird Named Isidore   116
Lisa Ress
Household Rules. Farwell Avenue, Chicago, 1946   118
Irene Reti
I Never Knew I Was Jewish   119
Jane Schapiro
The Tourist   124
Dora Weeks
(untitled)   125
V. RAIN OF THE BLUE TATTOOS
Marvin Bell
The Extermination of the Jews   129
Marvin Bell
Getting Lost in Nazi Germany   130
Joseph Glazer
Drinking with the Nazis   131
William Heyen
The Numinous   133
David Lampert
Poem for Sophie   135
Lyn Lifshin
Hearing of Reagan's Trip to Bitburg   137
Christopher Millis
The IRT at Rush Hour   138
Gail Newman
An Anti-Semitic Demonstration   139
Karen Propp
Train Passage   140
Anne Ranasinghe
Auschwitz from Colombo   142
Anne Ranasinghe
Sinhala New Year 1975   144
Lisa Ress
Learning the Ropes. Custer Street. Evanston, 1949   146
Lisa Ress
The Visit, Auschwitz, 1971   147
David Shevin
What He Hated   148

Contents

Nancy Shiffrin
Anna's Dream   150
Alina Tugend
Every Few Months   151
C. K. Williams
A Day for Anne Frank   152
VI. WE ARE THE RAGING FIRE
Talia N. Bloch
While Bouncing the Shema Back and Forth in Shul   159
Susan Dambroff
Resistance   161
Charles Fishman
Not Only in the Six-Day War   165
William Heyen
To the Onlookers   166
Phyllis Kahaney
Germany, 1981   167
Rachel Loden
Conversations with Dr. M.   170
Seymour Mayne
In Memory of Aaron, Murdered Grandfather   172
Richard Michelson
Genuine Jewish Flesh   173
Amos Neufeld
Children of Night   175
C. K. Williams
Spit   176
Biographies   179
Acknowledgments   188
Index of Poets   190

Foreword

I find myself having to transfer the *location* of these poems in order to get a grip on them. I have to imagine that they are poems written not by Jews or about Jews and Germans, but by Armenian or Cherokee survivors, and I find myself then, I don't know why, able to perceive them more as poems, as works of art, may the dead forgive me, than as testimonies of unbearable suffering. As I grow older, and as I accumulate distance from the incredible events of the late thirties and forties I find that those events are not more and more acceptable, as they become part of history, but rather less and less so. I am overcome with amazement, grief, incredulity. I can't believe it happened, that the children were murdered, that humans so degraded other humans, that technology was the means, that a culture was wiped out. And I can't believe that I went on with my own life the way I did, that I entertained long hair and flowers and poesy, that I learned French, that I taught Hopkins and Keats and sat in chairs memorizing them, that I agonized over my own petty failures. How is it that I didn't give up this sweet life and go from city to city raging, explaining, blaspheming? How is it that I didn't travel through Germany and Poland, accusing and demanding? How is it that I didn't become a murderer, or at the very least, a suicide? How is it that Jews in America and Argentina and France can go on with their ordinary lives, preparing for professions, memorizing a little script for the Bar Mitzvah? And how is it that Germans can return to normalcy, and how is it that the Christians can go on preparing themselves so exquisitely for paradise, as if they had not forgotten something, and how is it that the state and people of Israel can proceed with politics as usual in the face of the Covenants, and oppression, and even bigotry, in the face of Jewish history?

15

What are Holocaust poems, and what demand, and what freedom, did the Holocaust allow? Is there a unique dispensation that frees the poet of the normal or typical constraints of good literature and that requires only that her or his feelings be intense? Or is it the opposite, that the Holocaust poem, given its nature, must be better, *qua* poem, than another? Do only aesthetic considerations prevail (if they ever only do) or is it sacrilege to ask that of the poem? What is intensity, passion, deep feeling, anger, anyhow, in a poem? Aren't these things realized only when the poem is well written, beautiful? Do all the ancient issues regarding political poetry prevail, or are we beyond such issues here?

There are two things to say, or perhaps three. One is that, just as mad Ireland (according to Auden) drove Yeats into poetry, so did the Holocaust drive dozens of Jews there. A second is that it became the subject matter of many who, though poets, would otherwise have been writing about something else. The third is that though it (the Holocaust) made the poetry of some—even many—vivid, even overwhelming, it made the poetry of others, believe it or not, vapid, sentimental, even uninteresting. Perhaps that is because so many who wrote about the Holocaust weren't poets, or weren't thinking (or acting) as poets when they wrote their Holocaust poems. Perhaps it is because the subject is so overwhelmingly difficult to write about. How do you get distance, leverage, on the unspeakable, the unentertainable? Isn't it in the very nature of poetry to always reserve a place for hope? Isn't that reserve, that reservoir, what poetry is, and is about? Can there be business as usual—shall I say "art as usual"—with its restorations and its redemptions? Is there, indeed, room for more than one absolutely hopeless poem in each poet? Célan's "Death Fugue," if it is absolutely hopeless, is, as far as I know, the only poem he wrote that overcame the strictures, although its incredible music, and its drum beat, which is pure tragedy, and its great bitterness, which means deep intelligence and deep irony, are artistic qualities this side of the entrance to death and nothingness.

The poems in this anthology are by "second generation" poets, children of Holocaust survivors, Stewart Florsheim explains in his preface. There are memories of the camps, sometimes ordinary domestic details that by their very telling create a pathos and a horror; there are photographs of survivors, and nonsurvivors; there are visits to the new bland memoryless Germany; there are philosophic and mythic poems; there are dramatic and historical ones. If anything, there is a shying away from the sheer horror. What can one do, shout and bring the dead back? If anything, there is a kind of helplessness, perhaps even passivity. Maybe that's the only response. Or maybe it's that words themselves are so inappropriate, that they can never summon up the absolute cruelty, the orderliness, the insanity of the experience. For words, normally, can *create* the experience, whether it be fiction or poetry, out of nothing, as it were, and it is in the words and the images, in the created narrative, that the tension and the drama and the tragedy come to exist. But here it is history that precedes the poetry. And it is a history heretofore undreamed of, and it stands as an overwhelming force not only greater than, but indifferent to, literature. The very function, the very value, of literature is called into question. Can even great and beautiful words redeem the experience—was that not what Célan himself finally thought?

Unless we realize that the purpose of words is not just to redeem the past, but to explain it, elaborate upon it, talk to it, reason, scold, complain, ignore it, recreate it, repair it. Silence is the enemy; it has always been. Silence, and good manners. We must keep talking, even if we spit, and once or twice in a lifetime a poem will come. It is enough. Wilfred Owen said "the poetry is in the pity." He seemed to speak exquisitely for the unheroic of World War I, and we thought, for many years after, that he spoke exquisitely, and elegantly, for the decades after the war too. Perhaps that *credo* applies to Holocaust poetry too. I don't know. I'd like to say "the poetry is in the anger" or "in the bitterness" or "in the amazement." But there is anger and bitterness and amazement in Owen's poems, as well as pity, and in Rosenberg's poems too, that Rosenberg who wrote of "God's malodorous brain" and called him by the name of "rotting God." I am grateful to these poets for what they've done. A few of these poems are of a beauty and an order that is extraordinary. All of them will help us account for those years. It is not that we will either forget or reclaim those years because of these poems; it is not that the poems will even make that past bearable. It is that, in our greatest loss, we have a victory.

Gerald Stern

Preface

The idea for this book first came to me in a dream. But for years before that, I was writing poetry that was about being a child of Holocaust survivors. The dream spurred me; I decided to see if other children of the second generation were writing poetry about their lives and if any collections of their work had been published. I found books by and about victims and survivors, but virtually nothing by or about their children.

I sent out flyers soliciting poetry and prose to Holocaust groups, universities, and individual writers; I sent press releases to the major Jewish newspapers and periodicals around the United States, Israel, and parts of the English-speaking world including Canada, the United Kingdom, and Australia; and I placed ads in a few writers' magazines. The response was overwhelming. Over a period of approximately four months, I collected well over two hundred manuscripts containing about fifty stories and over one thousand poems. To keep the book to a manageable size, I decided to limit it to poetry.

It is difficult to establish who exactly comprises the second generation. The term generally refers to those individuals whose parents or family were in the camps, in hiding, fighting with the partisans, or had to flee Europe because of the Nazi regime. The book is organized by the major themes in the lives of the second generation, themes I derived from my own life and from the lives of people I know.

Although most of the poems in this book have been written by Jews, there is also work by non-Jews, including one writer whose family was involved with the Gestapo. The biographies in the back of the book generally include a reference to the poet's relationship to the Holocaust.

This book is also written for the many oppressed people in the world today who are faced with daily injustices and, in the worst cases, the threat of annihilation. Let us hope the poetry that their children write will not be full of ghosts.

Special thanks to the following people for their help and support: David Lampert, Mary Maher, J. D. Cloer, Jennifer Krebs, Jazan Higgins, Judy Rosloff, the members of Generation to Generation, and countless others who helped me along the way. Part of the proceeds from this book will be donated to Amnesty International and the Union of Councils for Soviet Jews to help them continue their very important work.

I
Assembling the Dead

Stephen Berg

Desnos Reading the Palms of Men
on Their Way to the Gas Chambers

> Our suffering would be unbearable if
> we couldn't think of it as a passing and
> sentimental disorder
> —Robert Desnos, March 28, 1944,
> Buchenwald

Maybe I should go back to the white leather
sofa and bull terrier
of my childhood, when my grandfather died,
but I can't.
It rained and there were beaks of light.
Who was it
picking my hand up where it hung
against my naked thigh?
What matters is how we act before we die,
whether we have a joke ready
and can make all the terrified sad faces
around us laugh and weep,
whether we can make everyone kiss.
Who was it? Who holds us here?
Whom should we touch?

You squeeze my hand.
The orchestra's notes from across the road
weave upward in the smoke,
the frozen eyes, the brown angular light
off center, rows, stacks, glasses
without anyone's eyes behind them
and nothing except
the smile of a boot,
the eyes of gloves,
the mouth of a belt

23

and the holes.
Holes.
I squeeze your hand.

You don't love anyone.
I'm sorry. You never loved anyone.
Probably it's because your planets
are mixed, or Jewish.
But there's a cross down by the wrist
on the edge of the mound of Venus
and lines tangling violently
along the third finger.
You're a sexual person.
Still, those lines webbed
under the thumb are bright.
The agony is false.
The earth has been here beneath us
less than an hour
and we are shuffling forward.
Nobody looks at us.
Say anything,
say we are somewhere else,
each violin has
long curved eyes
tilted seaward and up
like your hand in mine.

And yours, little boy with dark brown eyes,
is wetter than the fake soup
of urine and grass the Nazis give us.
You hide your penis fearfully
behind it, making a pathetic cup
while the other hand dangles
like a noose
that will open on no one,
close on no one.
But I predict one last moment of

incredible joy
when you see yourself melt
into the hundreds gasping around you,
and the doors are pulled
and the gas sighs once, reminding
the Father of you.

Nothing is lost. One guard sprouts wings
in his sleep. He is presented a robe of
spun blonde hair and a throne
of tiny nuggets.
In the morning on the parade ground
he opens his fly and prays for us
and is shot
and chopped up for the dogs.
But the next night he returns,
an amputated wing
branding its shadow in miniature
on twelve foreheads.

Like a blind clown I dance between
rifles and the laughter of kings,
and it must be my withered cock and balls,
the color of stone walls,
that cause so much happiness
in the ranks,
as I stumble through the prisoners to hold them,
needing to touch as many as I can
before I go.

There's a shallow hole over the bed
on the wall behind my head
where my dreams live on
after I have waked and knelt
and bled
thousands of times.
I look into it and if I concentrate

I see bodies decorated with
God's toil and ashes.
They drift
into the mouths and eyes
of the living
until there is nothing
but children
like us
here.

Shaggy grains of frost
cling to the ground.
The barracks glitter, the sky hugs
itself like a girl whose arms
have been hacked off, and the wire
hums invisibly in the night air except when a
strand goes white for a second
from no source.
O I want to be that thread, tiny
barrier, bodiless vein, line
that the wind reads.
When I chew on what looks like a finger
and tastes like sour wine
I remember you running, stretching your arms out
to be caught or to fling yourself
through space
until your laughter choked in the sand.
I remember nothing.

You ask me why.
I stand facing you
and speak your name,
whatever it is.
Your name over and over
like a lullaby
until we kiss.
I put my hand on your breast.

It is beautiful, and ugly,
and as empty
as we will be soon.
Lights begin passing
in your eyes
like cities going to sleep
or like those thick lamps on the masts
of fishing boats.
I love you more than I
have loved anyone.
You touch my hair and cry.

Are you different from the one
I just touched? Who are you?
Everyone looks so young suddenly
as if this were the beginning
of the world.
Everything is as silent as this hand
laid up in my palm,
except for a slight hissing somewhere.
What would you say if I spoke?
I will marry a beautiful woman
named Youki,
have children, a cottage
in the forest near Compiègne
and live many years?
I will marry and have children.

Sometimes a message flutters down,
and someone picks it up
and reads:

then goes back home.
The wheels clack.

Unbearable, the wrong parents, the sun
funneling down like the wings

of judgment. Love suffers.
                    I
dance in any direction now,
kissing the guards, soothing their faces
with my torn hands, singing like a child
after a long illness
who is here, here and here,
knowing you by the lost warmth
of your hands
in Philadelphia, Cape May,
New York, wherever I could not be.
Who is it?
I slide under the uniforms
and fill them,
and as I swim the sorrow and depth
of a stranger's blood, of
a belly held in by a bulletproof vest,
I know it was not a mistake
to be here.

I am my sister, but I have none.
My brother, but I have none.

Living men, what have you done?
In a strand
of invisible scorched nerve
scenes we won't remember
never stop flashing toward us,
unreceived,
like us.
The last wisps of gas
rise from our sleeves

and what I danced is danced again where
you smile about love
and eat with friends
the last smile is smiled first

and I am both of them
on the last mouth

and I am the light you see by
fingers tracing the breast
a cloud chilling the street suddenly
what you need, say, lie down
next to in hours
of common terror
I am the face
touch touch

and who it is is who it is

a boot's O empties itself eternally
as radiant in the holiness
of presence as
any

I go back
and can't
but I hear myself
call the flesh
call what I love
what I love is not listening

Don't you hear it?
It says "The pain will soon be over"
It says "The lovely season is near"

Don't you hear it?

Stewart J. Florsheim

Real Chocolate

> The practice of gang rape of female
> prisoners by soldiers was a common
> occurrence in the camps. . . .
> —Anonymous inmate at Auschwitz

They lured me out of the barracks
with promises of chocolate
and words like "Schätzchen,"
but the other women knew,
and called me soldier's whore
even before they heard the noises outside.
I knew as well,
but hunger has a way of changing you,
of causing you to forget who you are.
Funny, how there can be hope in desperation.

They threw the chocolate on the ground
and laughed: "da, fress." I lunged for it,
and tasted mud. "Dreh dich rum, Judenschwein."
I saw big black boots, pairs and pairs,
and the ground was so muddy,
it seemed to give way to my body.
I hiked up my prisoner's garb and spread my legs.
They were so light and opened so easily
that I thanked God because I knew
I wouldn't resist.
This body is no longer mine, this hunger;
at last, there is no reason to fight.

I wonder now if their desire for me
was a desire for death,
fucking a bald woman who was only skin and bones,
whose only salvation would be a cup of watery soup

for dinner, a slice of stale bread,
and maybe, if the soldiers wanted her again,
this time, a piece of real chocolate.

William Heyen

Blue

> They were burning something. A lorry
> drew up at the pit and delivered its
> load—little children. Babies! Yes, I saw
> it—saw it with my own eyes . . . those
> children in the flames. . . . I pinched
> my face. Was I still alive? Was I awake?
> I could not believe it. . . . Never shall I
> forget the little faces of the children,
> whose bodies I saw turned into
> wreaths of smoke, beneath a silent
> blue sky.
> —Elie Wiesel

    To witness, to
   enter this
essence, this
silence, this
  blue, color
  of sky, wreaths
    of smoke, bodies
  of children blue
in their nets
of veins: a lorry
  draws up at the pit
  under the blue sky where
    wreaths rise. These
  are the children's bodies, this
our earth. Blue. A lorry
draws up at the pit
  where children smolder. The sky
  deepens into blue, its
    meditation, a blue
  flame, the children
smolder. Lord of blue,

blue chest and blue brain,
a lorry of murdered children
draws up at the pit. This
happened, this
happens, Your
sign, children
flaming in their rags, children
of bone-smolder, scroll
of wreaths on Your blue
bottomless sky, children
rising wreathed
to Your blue lips.

William Heyen

The Trains

Signed by Franz Paul Stangl, Commandant,
there is in Berlin a document,
an order of transmittal from Treblinka:

248 freight cars of clothing,
400,000 gold watches,
25 freight cars of women's hair.

Some clothing was kept, some pulped for paper.
The finest watches were never melted down.
All the women's hair was used for mattresses, or dolls.

Would these words like to use some of that same paper?
One of those watches may pulse in your own wrist.
Does someone you know collect dolls, or sleep on human hair?

He is dead at last, Commandant Stangl of Treblinka,
but the camp's three syllables still sound like freight cars
straining around a curve, Treblinka,

Treblinka. Clothing, time in gold watches,
women's hair for mattresses and dolls' heads.
Treblinka. The trains from Treblinka.

Barbara Helfgott Hyett

Assembling the Dead at Dachau

This is where they begin:
like the angels who watched
over Hansel and Gretel,
one nazi stands at the head,

his fingers twisting
the coarse cloth of a sleeve.
How blue the eyes of a man
whose obedience is absolute.

One nazi stands at the feet,
holding the piss-soaked cuffs,
the body—a sandbag
in the bloodied hands

of the men who lift it,
who swing it
back and forth, back
and forth, the long spine

sweeping dust, hipbones
clacking like schrapnel
in a porcelain bowl.
All Jews weigh the same.

Now they let go: the husk
of a man sailing onto a truckbed,
hand flapping like a sparrow
trapped in the rags of his clothes.

Lyn Lifshin

Crystal Night

windows slashed
like skin pulled
tight   frozen with a
stone   slammed thru
it   smashed blue

glass   crystal   a
whole lake of ice
a plane crashes
into   smashed
tea cups   bowl of

glass   glass
shattering in the
night   something like
a mirror walked
into they came   beat

people up   blue
jars   the glass piled
in an alley calf
deep. All night the
sound of ice in

the branches poking
holes in the roof
A warning   stained
glass from the
synagogue slashed

plum   peach   cherry
frosting over in
the chill NOvember
light   an arm
torn   bleeding

a whole family
in shards and this
just the beginning

Lyn Lifshin

Seeing the Documentary by the British Liberating Bergen-Belsen

the bodies like driftwood
tangling   naked as
marble or roots of
trees suddenly torn
from the earth that
held it   like the
scalped shrunken heads
of the polish scientist
who tried to run
unreal as the man
shot when he chewed
earth to get out of
the cell for air   the
bottom half of his body
burning   bodies stacked
like wood   a cross
dangling   child frozen
into a breast   his
legs cut off   wrinkled
little hot dogs

Lyn Lifshin

Bergen-Belsen 1945

the children ate
whatever we gave them
we got clothes from
another town   the
new sweaters and
skirts were symbolic
meant new hope   they
put them on with
pride   there were
more than 220 children
still alive   to them
the new clothes were
mysterious   one soldier
said in April that
no one could believe
humans had done this

Richard Michelson

Interrogation

> Pregnant women were ordered to
> stand an hour on one leg. If their foot
> touched ground, they were told, their
> stomachs would be pierced.
> —H.O., Treblinka, 1943

We lift our legs.
Dogs peeing. O Pavlova: In the mausoleum
that is my womb, my child crouches
like the dying swan, while I spin
on point, pirouette until, like Elijah,
I begin to rise.
Dirt breeds lice,
lice typhus. How improbably long
our bodies remain alive. Today, twice
I have escaped selection. My legs, grown strong,
balance against death like a dancer
frozen between question and answer,
performance and applause.
My art
is inseparable from my grief. The earth,
like a davening Jew, starts to sway. My heart
teeters, doubles its beat. Each breath
in Hell is an act of resistance.
I tell my heavy feet to dance.

Richard Michelson

Faraway Landscape

> pen and ink uncovered in Buchenwald
> —1944

An artist in our midst. Fool, I tell myself, why risk
what little life you've left to steal him ink
and pad. He gives no thanks. I think
he thinks it natural. I have my task

as he has his. I've come to hate
his scratching late each night while dead men rest
their bones and fathers beat their breasts.
Etched in crusts of bread I find small trees,

all Eden carved into a rotting scrap
of meat. It matters not that starved men eye
each other's flesh. He hears their cries
but will not document their pain. Apples,

he draws instead, knowing each line could be his last;
still he must see Palestine, that faraway landscape
take shape once more, as if he could escape
this world, imagining the future or the past.

Anne Ranasinghe

Holocaust 1944

To my mother

I do not know
In what strange far off earth
They buried you;
Nor what harsh northern winds
Blow through the stubble,
The dry, hard stubble
Above your grave.

And did you think of me
That frost-blue December morning,
Snow-heavy and bitter,
As you walked naked and shivering
Under the leaden sky,
In that last moment
When you knew it was the end,
The end of nothing
And the beginning of nothing,
Did you think of me?

Oh I remember you my dearest,
Your pale hands spread
In the ancient blessing,
Your eyes bright and shining
Above the candles
Intoning the blessing
Blessed by the Lord. . . .

And therein lies the agony,
The agony and the horror
That after all there was no martyrdom

But only futility—
The futility of dying
The end of nothing
And the beginning of nothing.
I weep red tears of blood.
Your blood.

Enid Shomer

Women Bathing at Bergen-Belsen

April 24, 1945

Twelve hours after the Allies arrive
there is hot water, soap. Two women bathe
in a makeshift, open-air shower while nearby
fifteen thousand are flung naked into mass graves
by captured SS guards. Clearly legs and arms
are the natural handles of a corpse. The bathers,
taken late in the war, still have flesh
on their bones, still have breasts. Though nudity was
a death sentence here, they have undressed,
oblivious to the soldiers and the cameras.
The corpses push through the limed earth like upended
headstones. The bathers scrub their feet, bending
in beautiful curves, mapping the contours
of the body, that kingdom to which they've returned.

II
Family Album

Karen Alkalay-Gut

Life Goes On

"Life goes on",
said Ronald Reagan at Bitburg

Mine began the last day of the blitz
because my mother stopped having abortions.

My brother and I—coaxed from aging parents
so surprised at survival only birth could give proof.

What would they have been—those brothers and sisters—
that our mother, fleeing, flushed from her womb?

Annette Bialik Harchik

Requiem

Your names ring clearly,
carefully through my mind. . . .
Sheyna, Pesach,
Chana, Yankel.
Your names my legacy:
my grandparents,
my aunts,
my uncles.
Your names echo
in my heart,
Helena, Gitl,
Miriam, Kreindl,
echo in my skin.
Echo hollow vowels
and consonants,
naming the names.
Duvid, Nissum,
Zukkin, Shmuel.
Names
name
themselves,
not flesh.

I picture you
before me,
so strangely dressed
in the fashions of your time:
aged grandfolk in wrinkled clothes
stand stiff, stern, and loving;
handsome uncles
smiling in sunlight;

tender aunts awkward
before the camera.
I ache to touch your faces,
and caress each feature;
to pull my fingers through
dark thicknesses of your hair.
I long to meet
the steady gaze of your eyes,
to meet—you.

Your names whisper clearly,
carefully through my mind,
tagging lost people
like missing baggage.
Sheyna, Pesach,
Chana, Yankel.
Helena, Gitl,
Miriam, Kreindl.
Duvid, Nissum,
Zukkin, Shmuel.
I am unable to claim
the tickets to your lives.
Who would you each
be to me
now?
You who are not here
and yet
ever
with me.

William Heyen

For Hermann Heyen

(d. 1941 over Russia)

Hermann, the Channel was blue-green
when you banked your plane and headed
back. But the Stuka's wing,
down which you sighted the countries you hated,
shone brilliant as medals,
didn't it? Your plane seemed
almost to be on fire, didn't it?

My Nazi uncle, you received the letters
my father still talks and wonders about—
the ones in which he told you to bail out
over England and plead insanity.
You got the letters, didn't you?
But you kept saying you'd land in London
with the rest of your squadron,

in a few months, when the war was over,
of course. Of course. But they needed you
in Russia, didn't they? And the few
who bailed out there were met by peasants
with pitchforks and scythes, weren't they?

Anyway, your plane blew up, for a moment,
like a sun; your dust bailed out all over.

Phyllis Kahaney

Pogrom

At the church they killed a pig once.
They lit a fire, slit its throat,
then stood in circles, drinking beer.
While dinner sizzled someone
as a joke invited Aunt Fruma.
She arrived in white, her black hair plaited.

Ten years later a village boy
dressed as a soldier beats on her door.
Outside are others, each
with a gun to gather one by one
the dark-eyed women whose husbands
and fathers are gone to war.
Snow covers their footprints.

In the moonlight the steeple looms huge
through trees. Fruma pauses, remembering.
The women enter, arm in arm.
When the door is bolted, Fruma knows
how smoke will rise through doors
and ruby windows and, finally, the roof.

Sharon Kessler

Family Secrets

My waiting time is over. I absolve you
with a quick mumbled prayer for the lost
Sabbath guests of the imagination. Return, then,
to your gruesome demise. Immortality your wish,
you let this happen. So our sons carry
your name's heavy baggage on their backs.
God help them if they have to run.
Now tell the truth.
Everyone said you were coming, and you're late.
They made me wait. I watched for you,
I was too small to reach the window,
but I waited, grew, you didn't come, yet
I am waiting for you always, and
once, at the Museum of Modern Art,
I saw you cross the street; I followed,
to the subway, I never met you, but I'm waiting still,
in schoolyards, at carnivals and discotheques,
department stores and movies, redwood forests, and now
I tell you it's enough. Put your hands up.
Make us a signal. We've learned to read the smoke.
Stand up like an honest dead man
un zug ins vas hat getrafen.

Sharon Kessler

Names the Dead Speak

> No one sleeps in this room without the
> dream of a common language.
> —Adrienne Rich

My father, who loves my mother,
does not call her in the language
of her birth. She still hears
how her mother shouted from the window
when she begged, Mama, Mama,
throw down a penny, *warf arup a penny.*
The child who became my mother
went to the candy store
in a language I hardly speak.
My own children will teach her
ice cream flavors in the language
prophets spoke, as I named flavors
for my grandmother in the English
my children will not know.
The word for *chocolat* is the same
for my mother and me, but not the names
my father called us, not Harriet,
not Sharon, nor the names
denied us in exile, not Hadassah,
not Shoshana, nor the names
my grandmother gave us,
Hoodis, Raisl, her mothers' names,
names she won't live to call my children.
In a bastard tongue, a foreign tongue,
a holy tongue, I'll choose
all her names for my children,
in the only common language,
names the dead speak.
We are forbidden to give our children
the names of the living.

Denyse Kirsch

Dvora

Today
to be a Jew in Israel
is to carry in your heart a lifelong debt
and obligation
to those who could not come.
Six million died
and with their death destroyed
a soul and spirit of generations.
I was not there—then—
thank God
and cannot write of how it was.
But all the while
the echoes of the screams of those who were
beat in my head
and with them
hers
for whom I was named.

Steven C. Levi

Abbienti

There is a photograph in my father's
study which shows three generations
posing casually in the spring sun of 1932.

The grandparents dominate the center
of the photo. Gathered about them are
their three children and a ghost in the
shadows. Oldest was Rodolfo, sizing up
the camera, arrogant, as if he were pressed
for time, impatient for appearance but practical
for politics. He is not pressed for time now.

There is Amalia and her two sons, Mario and Fausto.
There was Maria with her two sons. The two husbands,
Vittorio and Ernesto, casually eye the photographer.
Enzo, the son of Maria and Ernesto, stares into
the camera with the eyes of a wizard. His brother,
Ferruccio, in children's light summer clothes with
white knee socks, perches on the railing.

In the shadows is Cesare, dressed in the uniform
of an Italian artillery officer. The blood is gone
from his uniform and he is sitting casually in the
empty chair. As a spectre he is as he was in life,
silent.

These were the *abbienti* of a distant age, a passing
generation, a forgotten culture. Affluent Jews
in the land of the Catholic. Lawyers and managers
in a city where calloused hands were endemic and

cauliflowered brains raised black sleeved arms in
salute.

Serenely they all look toward the photographer
with the casualness of a life of intellectual
ease. The walls of the garden protect them
from the riff-raff of the street. There
would be no castor oil for this crew,
yet.

Seymour Mayne

Zalman

The name was curiously given.
Both families agreed the firstborn's
would be chosen from the mother's side.
Her father's name? No, he may still be alive—
May '44—if the Nazis hadn't killed him yet.
Who knew of his end then?
                                    But the mother's mother,
Zlateh—she who had married twice
and amassed money and means—
a boy named after a woman? Was it a forbidden thing?
And the name rooted from the Marranos
and hidden observance: Zalman;
Suleiman—did they know of the Turkish origins?
Not drawn from the Pentateuch,
no, a name of the orient, the eastern Diaspora
and linked in the beginning, the first consonant,
with a grandmother whose only lasting image:
the block of stone carved with Hebrew
in Bialystok's cemetery and her youngest son,
the uncle, standing there in the photo
just weeks before Poland fell—
the rest of her brood caught in a burning synagogue
before they could buy passage to New Jersey or Montreal.
She was dead then, her ears stopped
with that terrible silence marking its way
from the din of outrage—the flames licked the night
and the polish and german murderers
prepared for a Saturday night off, the air incensed
with smoke of scrolls and flesh.
Enough, we begin again, the father said, name him.
She will live.
                    —On their lips and in my face.

57

Mark Nepo

The Oil of Her Hands

(For Rifkah)

I wonder about Rifkah, my grandmother's sister,
returning the steamship tickets, wanting Rumania,
finding Treblinka or Buchenwald.

I wonder when she realized obedience was less than smoke.
And how many young Aryans, uncomfortable
with the muggy straps of their helmets,
how many looked at her supple cold hips
and thought, "Could we not spare her?
Could we not stop and chat or rub
something beside the grease of triggers?"

                I wonder did she fight
or slip her clothes like a scented robe
descending the ditch like a siren who has lost
her power to bewitch the slowest wolf.

Amos Neufeld

Family Album

My father stands in the picture
with his parents, brothers and sisters.
(The gas and sealed cattle-cars
are still two years away.) They smile
not knowing this is the last time
they will be gathered happily together,
that nothing guards their world,
that sky will be all that remains.

Their eyes rest peacefully
on one another and on the camera
while tomorrow winds its arms
and twists tighter round their necks.
Yet it is still too early
to see the black boots coming:
smoke floats carelessly from a cigarette
and children go to summer camp.

We see them—not yet lost,
standing on the precipice of wind and fire,
their image of vanished innocence,
captured and in our memory engraved.
Still they stand, unsuspecting,
composed, like any other happy family,
while their black and white world rushes toward . . . .
is already on the final page.

Amos Neufeld

Pictures and Stories

I never knew you,
Never heard your voice,
Your laughter,
Your love or your generational wisdom
Which you would have passed on to your grandchild—
Just pictures and stories.

I could never kiss you,
Never hold your hand,
Your heart,
Your life or your thoughtful years
With which you would have blessed your grandchild—
Just pictures and stories.

I only knew two sepia photographs
Recovered from a street at night
And scattered stories
And tears, streaming from death to life,
Which shall never revive you.

One grave in a closed land
And three in the open sky
In whose shades of blue I search for you.
But the clouds drift by teeming with millions.

All those sad staring eyes—
A generation's, raining down on us,
Filling our hearts with a heavy hurt.
All those sad eyes above
And too few open hearts below
Prophesy a chilling flood for the ages.

Evelyn Posamentier

Being Modern in Jerusalem

> (in memory of my mother, Alice
> Posamentier, and her mother, my
> grandmother, Gisela Epstein Fisk)

gisela, i went to the wall.
your daughter has seen the snapshots
of me in jerusalem.
gisela, i crammed a prayer into the wall
perhaps as you were crammed
toward god
in that lightless dark somewhere
where your sabbath lights dimmed
in the 40's, in the old country
when this time the ancient amalek came disguised
as pairs of polished boots with
wild dogs straining at their leashes.
your daughter has seen the snapshots
of me, her future, seated mute
on a stone, decades later
outside, on the hills of jerusalem, your
monument, *yad vashem.*
there was another teenage girl
seated beside me, a second
or third generation american jew.
while she wept, she stared at me
& then quietly asked
why aren't you crying?
all your grandparents, she sobbed, then wept
again & again
for the other millions of voices.
soon she pulled herself together
& snapped my photo with the instamatic.

gisela, your daughter
has seen this snapshot of
her daughter: cool in the desert
light, solemn & new, sunglasses concealing
my eyes.

Evelyn Posamentier

The Hungarian Medical Student: 1928

perhaps he is of medium height.
he is, of course, bespectacled.
& shy; the ever-present textbook
gently concealed in his grasp
as the trolley is ridden to the university
& back to the furnished, rented room.
no doubt, the landlady is thoroughly taken
by his unobtrusive politeness, his well-
polished, but as of yet
unaffordable future.
then boy meets girl.
they meet at a synagogue social function
for young adults.

he is new to vienna, serious
with the prospect of diligent study.
the city, standing on its own history, swells with glamour.
she is 16, with the instilled
& almost involuntary ghetto determination
for a correct future.
she learns to clothe herself in fashions
purchased for her by a relatively well-off uncle.
she inhales the magic of this golden city:
she cloaks herself in it.

the hungarian medical student, more frequently now, asserts
his intentions for their betrothal with a quiet insistence:
he has met the right girl.
he has memorized her every attribute
with the precision one devotes to the bone by bone
absorption of an anatomical chart:

he is sincere.
there is a picnic in the vienna woods.
a tablecloth is laid out, she sits in the clearing
as women in their time do:
demure & marriageable, two steps behind a future which
only i, the future, can decode from the sepia photo.
& he lies beside her, gazing up as a suitor
does, at her buddhistic pose, through
his wire-rimmed spectacles, his narrow frame
unfattened by the crumpled suit
covering it.
what is in her eyes?
i squint to see, to establish this algebraic X
in her eyes, so that I might complete
my mother's equation.

i don't know what happened to him she says.
the photos, once again, are crammed into the shoe box
& returned to the closet.
i just couldn't go through with it she adds from the kitchen
*i just couldn't marry him, so he went back to hungary, from which
i don't believe he managed to survive.*

Lisa Ress

The Family Album

Some pages have eyes, some mouths. They desire.
Put a platter on. I want to dance at the Stadtpark Café.
They have papers to complete. Tax records haunt them.
Their secretaries, still on leave, were never notified when to return.
Each page has an aura of surprise.
I was just putting dinner on the table. Here is the book
I promised Max. Sidi has not spoken to her father.

They stare at me, move their lips.
Alive or dead, they ask,
their worried, torn-up faces stuck to the page.
I try to help. I call up music,
wide brass notes that tear them free.
We put our arms back, and our faces, lace our flesh.
We are one body, whole.
The city walls keep time, they spin with us,
one clamorous gold mote, dancing away.

Marie Syrkin

My Uncle in Treblinka

My uncle, man of science in Berlin,
Grew old in honor
Having prospered.

In the evil days,
With neither work nor visa,
He wrote:
I spend my time
Solving problems and reading Scripture,
I seek truth.

The Germans led my uncle to Treblinka.
He went with his prayers and equations,
His psalms and logarithms.
At the door of the slaughter-house
Both were with him:
The angels at his side.

God of Israel,
Light of Reason,
In the chamber of gas, in the pit of lime,
Did my uncle, gentle and hard of hearing,
Feel their pinions over his head?

To the seat of justice,
Where prayers are heard and problems solved,
I, ignorant alike of Hebrew and mathematics,
Send these words for my uncle,
Murdered in Treblinka.

Evelyn Wexler

The Governess

I know what I am not.

Not family.
  Not servant.
  Not guest.

Yet engraved napkin ring says I have
  a place here as I sit in my own outside
    with attentive, table-tennis face.

I wear the special occasion blue dress.
  And the brooch mother, with imprisoned tongue
    and fugitive eyes, gave me

the time I was banished for loving
  a jew. In father's eye
    only the monocle glistened.

I lived with a jew.
  He was a poet and so died
    before the rest.

Vienna's waltzes finished, like the
  lace ribbons spanning Buda to Pest,
    I link the balky boy, to family.

Sometimes a child with ashen eyes
  watches me from behind the shadows.
    At night, when I creep into the kitchen for warm milk

to quiet menopausal maunderings,
   I see ovens in those eyes and shut my own.
   There are nights when I cannot sleep from her weeping.

Her sighs crack the walls of the room
   I share with the boy. He sleeps the heavy
   sleep of the unhearing, dreaming puffs of future.

Last night she slipped under the crack in the door
   and crawled into me. Sobs stilled, she slept.
   Europe died within my womb.

      I know what I am not.

Merra Young-Prottengeier

Lithuanian Grandmother

You stand in your kitchen,
round and short,
perspiration on your face.
You cook with a stone oven
and open hearth.
Smells of fresh bread,
tzmisis, szoldn.

Smells waft from your decade
into mine. Pass through unseen
the dark Holocaust curtain.
Take you from me,
before I am born.

Named after your name,
no picture of you exists.
Your son, my father, tells me
I resemble you.

I know you guide me,
from your kitchen;
from your star in heaven.
Tell me what spices to put
in my soups.
Whisper to me in Yiddish:
"Merele, my Merele."
Your hand kisses the mezuzah
with its hidden prayers,
on my doorpost.

III
Far from Auschwitz

BonniLee

White Candles

I used to watch her
          pacing
back
and forth
cleaning, crying
crying, screaming
With these forces this woman
my Mother
kept her heart
beating.

She was always
inside
          bitter
sweet regrets
She made herself to be
          an old woman
when I still needed
to look up
to her
So many years nonsmiling
chiseled
          fine   grooved   lines
around her lips
drooping.

I used to watch her
always in the kitchen
removing gold speckles
from the formica counters,
or else she'd be at the front door

searching
with eyes
          unfocused
arms dangling
with no place to go
My Mother she stood alone
          her sadness pressed
onto the cool glass
of the front
door.

I remember
how she used to look
stooped
over the white candles
bought special
for Shabbot
A clean handkerchief
hastily
poised upon her head
          Every week
she'd search the junk drawer
for a copy
of the prayer
recited
          for centuries
Her outstretched arms
embraced
the space
making it sacred
allowing color
          and tranquility
into her eyes
          for   one   moment
as she'd light
the candles.

I remember
how the house smelled
after my mother lit the match
with her head
inside an oven
      filled
            with gas
And the neighbors poured in
the stench
of her private holocaust
causing them all
to remember.

Cheryl J. Fish

Work and Worry

In memory of Rebecca Schiffer

You seemed older
you crossed at 12
the only one to be called

survivor working on demand
no questions, no time for yourself

you met him, younger than you
but he joked, you remembered
your mother at night
red hair like yours
leaning to kiss you
they said no one survived
but you did
you married him

became my grandmother
I heard about how tough
you were
saw for myself your little
hands could do anything
cook, sew, wash, scrape,
bond, soothe, scatter, pray

your words stung deeper
as you grew older
I could take it and love you
you aimed straight

little swollen feet that
slowed you down but
couldn't trip you

why aren't you married yet
what's wrong with your
personality? Then you helped
me pack my suitcase for my trip
so glad I asked for your help

slipping me money I smiled
I hated to believe you could suffer
your whole life for living

allowing yourself nothing
but work and worry
they kept you busy

until you died.

Stewart J. Florsheim

Weekend in Palm Springs

1
The pool light shimmers
from my parents' hotel room.
This is the new wealth,
the one after the years
in the small apartment that rocked
with the George Washington Bridge;
the years when money was so scarce
we never talked about it,
happily deceived by the steaks
my father brought home from work.
My parents did speak about
how proud they were never to accept a dime
when they came from Germany;
how they can still never waste any food
because the only thing grandfather wanted
when he wrote home from Dachau
was a stick of butter
to ease his nerves.

2
At the hotel spa,
the black man in the white gym suit
wraps a towel around me
as I emerge from the tub.
He tucks me in in the cooling room—
first, the fresh white sheet,
then a long bath towel.
I lie there naked, somewhat faint,
his long fingers wrapping me in a tight cocoon.
He pats my face dry, gently,

and I look up, surprised to see myself
so protected in his eyes.
He smiles, and I say, startled, thank you.
His teeth gleam as he laughs,
tells me, no, thank-*you;*
if it weren't for *you,*
I wouldn't be here.

3
Over dinner, my father asks me
if I overheard the German being spoken
around the pool. I tell him, no,
but still ask him, as I did when I was a boy,
if it's the right kind.
He says he's not sure,
there's the one jeweler from Salzburg,
but there are a few people
with numbers branded on their arms.
Did I see them?
He finishes his entire meal,
eats the ice-cream, too,
whether or not he is hungry,
if it's part of the daily special.
After dinner, we walk up and down the boulevard,
my parents quick to point out
the WASPs, Mexicans; all the non-Jews.
We stroll slowly, leisurely,
my father smiling as he points
to someone's T-shirt:
"Palm Springs, I love you."

Barbara Goldberg

Survivor

for Blanka

They say I should feed you,
child with gift the of tongues.
But darting through woods of dark pine
hounds chase the scent of sandals.

Days spent under cover
in a field of eiderdown,
my fingers search for traces
of my own lost mother.

At night, when the bulb shines through
the parchment, and I scrub
my body down with soap,
I think of her parting lace curtains
looking for Father to round the corner.

A small patch of pain presses against the North
side of this house. Here, by Union Turnpike,
a car is parked in the driveway.
We'd all fit in, all, if we had
to make a quick journey.
I keep a bar of gold under my pillow.

They bring you to me, my locket
clasped in your fist. I want
to feed you.

It's those spiked needles that scrape
against the glass, those shadows
that won't sleep behind the drapes.

It's that woodsman walking
through this forest
swinging his ax.

Annette Bialik Harchik

Earrings

A Bialik tradition back home   was
for a woman to wear   earrings
from birth to death.

Ears pierced in infancy   were
adorned in string;
small gold hoops for girlhood;
diamond studs with marriage.

When the trains pulled up
at Auschwitz
my mother was stripped, shorn,
and tattooed, leaving behind her   earrings
in a huge glittering pile of jewelry.

Under her wavy white hair,
her lobes hang heavy,
the empty holes
grown shut.

Lyn Lifshin

I Remember Haifa Being Lovely But

there were snakes in the
tent, my mother was
strong but she never
slept, was afraid of
dreaming. In Auschwitz
there was a numbness,
lull of just staying
alive. Her two babies
gassed before her, Dr.
Mengele, you know who
he is? She kept her
young sister alive
only to have her die
in her arms the night
of liberation. My mother
is big boned, but she
weighed under 80 lbs.
It was hot, I thought
the snakes lovely. No
drugs in Israel, no
food, I got pneumonia,
my mother knocked the
doctor to the floor
when they refused,
said I lost two in
the camp and if this
one dies I'll kill
myself in front of
you. I thought that
once you became a
mother, blue numbers
appeared mysteriously,
tattooed on your arm

Gail Newman

Photograph of Survivors

It doesn't look like him.
Doesn't look like my father.
His hair is thick and there is
a softness around the mouth
as if all his life has been gathering
up into this moment in which he sits

next to my mother, shirt open at the collar,
fingers pressed into her palm,

but she is gazing into the future
or into the past, eyes filmy
as a pond under algae, her lips

just slightly turned up. This is
as far as she can bring herself, for his sake,
quietly fighting to stay alive.

Gary Pacernick

Louie the Tailor

While I stuffed wrapping paper
Into boxes, Louie the tailor
Worked upstairs in the loft
At Jack's Haberdashery.
A tiny man with big blue
Watery eyes and a high-pitched
Heavily accented voice,
He stood behind the huge iron.
Steam rose to the ceiling
As Louie pressed out the wrinkles
In newly purchased garments.
The arm of the iron rose and fell
In a staccato beat, hissing
With heat. Just as hot to me
Was the nude Marilyn Monroe
Calendar pinned to the cracked wall
Behind Louie, who never seemed to notice it.
Louie, the proud husband and father,
Was happy to be pressing clothes
Upstairs in the steamy loft
At Jack's Haberdashery
Far, far from the ovens of Auschwitz.

Lisa Ress

Waving Her Farewell. Train Station, Vienna XV, 1939

It is not a trip to the Prater or Augarten to play.
On the train seat, a basket,
two rolls, the last butter. Behind her
massed parents, the platform blurred with coats.
Years forward she will waken still telling over faces of the dead.
The count, not finished at nightfall, awaits.
No one will like her dark looks.
She has tasks.
Inside her cupped palms, the city, thousand years,
the wailing shades.
She wails back,
sucked forward to the tunnel, sent
with weeping children into immigration sheds at Dover.
Someone else's life, she thinks. How mine?
Wiping the dirt from the window, a circle for her eye
and everywhere the tunnel
howling at both mouths.

Elizabeth Rosner

Souvenirs

Chocolate

My father is a chocolate hoarder. It is a family joke, this desperate need of his to have a stash of candy bars and various sweets hidden in a number of places around the house (in shoeboxes on high closet shelves, under piles of winter hats, behind bunches of unmatched socks, trapped between old bills and unanswered letters); he even has a drawer in his desk at work that is reserved for candy storage—an unexpected treasure chest we discovered on a childhood visit to his office. Whenever he returned from a business trip, whether he had been away for a few days or a couple of weeks, there was always a joyous reunion that involved the immediate ransacking of his suitcases (even my mother would join in); each time we managed to uncover a cluster of assorted chocolate bars, nougat candies, unfamiliar delights. My father would stand by the bed and watch our mad hunt, laughing I suppose at our gleeful rummaging and also at his own secret triumph; he had, no doubt, already stuffed his own pockets or hidden some morsels in his shaving kit.

I remember my mother making occasional passing remarks about his obsession with chocolate, something like "Your father never had sweets as a child" or some equally incomprehensible notion. Did he have a strict dentist? Or were his parents overly concerned about cavities? I didn't understand.

My father's cousin Tamara, now living in Holland, recently told me a story about the night before she left Germany with her parents, the last time she would see my father for many years. "I was five and he was nine," she recounted, "and he was terribly frightened. I remember it so very well, such a small, scared boy. My father tried to comfort him, saying 'Don't worry, your father will come back for you.' He gave him a chocolate bar and I thought 'No, no, he doesn't want the chocolate, he wants to come with us.'"

Barry Sternlieb

Survivor

He stands on the bridge
waiting for another
train to break
the surface of the north
and echo ties
below him, the past
finding itself
in the presence of steel
as engines pull miles
of freight toward New York.
He wants to hear the voices
reach again and again,
from German
into hope and ashes.

The last islands
of snow slowly fade
on the hills.
For wild geese, a migration
is over, but his years
are the color of flight,
dark as the captive
eyes he feels
burning through the boxcars.
The hours become names,
so his daughter
will find him reflective
as a thin March moon
watching the distant rails,
and she'll stay there awhile
before leading him back
to all that is left
for the darkness to give.

Morrie Warshawski

Sonia at 32

The lady never shakes free the ashes
of the dead. Dark clouds.
Dark cauliflower fists.
A birdbath full of urine. The fish

bladder that bubbles up and
bounces in the sink. I climb
the cherry tree for her this year,
watch the large rats dart

into the basement below, and
carry 5-gallon jars of fresh
clover honey up rickety
back stairs. This lady is

the witness who never forgets.
She hangs wet wash on the
line in a stiff wind against
a background of dust. She yells

at the dog catcher and cuts
chicken to the bone. She cries
long distance about this and
that. About the little man

who is her son. The little
son who is her husband. Over
and over she sings the song
her dead brother hummed hiding

behind their house, and holds
each breath as if to say,
"Don't Shoot!"

Florence Weinberger

Survivor

He knows the depths of smokestacks,
from their bleak rims down
their spattered walls, from their ash cones
to the bone-bottom ground.
Once he could see under skin,
inside the body, where deprivation
thins the blood of all desire
except hunger.
For years he wanted to forget
everything. He knows it is possible
to live only at the surface,
it is possible to work,
to marry and have daughters.
But his daughters
look like people he once knew,
and he dreams them.
He dreams them opening doors,
sending letters. When he wakes,
he knows he has been dreaming.
This year, he will show his daughters
where he was born. He will show them
the chimney, the iron gate,
the deep oven where his mother baked bread.

Florence Weinberger

He Wears Old Socks

He wears old socks,
pajamas full of holes,
saves shoes, saves
everything, stuffs
large amounts of food
in his cheeks, chews
slowly. So much is
his. This is how
he once survived.
Now he has means
to buy new socks,
eat in restaurants.
It isn't that old
habits die hard,
or even memories.
It's the way he
represents the dead,
with his own bones,
not knowing
where the others lie.

Will Wells

Beatings

She slings her rugs faithfully
over the clothesline to flog them
beyond cleanliness with a broom.

It rises with her pulse and each
measured thud—that barrage advancing
forever at the edge of consciousness.

The German regiment fanned out
across the vineyard, treading grapes
under hobnail boots, kicking up
an acrid dust to dwell in the eyes:
seeds of sorrow, dregs of defeat.

All summer the tanks clanked by,
churning dust devils to possess her
these years and nations later . . .

Children line the fence to ponder
such grim single-mindedness, the rumor
of an Old World that she repeats
in the muffled detonations of her dust.

IV

I Am Your American Child

Joan (Thaler) Dobbie

Forty Three Years After Hitler My Parents Visit Eugene

one day in the fall sun
my mom & dad
& ted & i
took a picnic
up on skinner's butte.

now ted, he speaks german
too, though he's not jewish
like my dad, with his white
einstein halo of hair,
and my mom

and me,
i spoke german as a baby
but i forgot.
my brother and sisters & i,
we grew up with forgetting.

the climb was slow;
we took it easy.
leaves rustled
because it hadn't started
raining yet.

ted pushed his bike up
so he could leave early
but he didn't leave
very early.
the sky was light.

we munched our avocado frenchbread
sandwiches & sipped apple juice
& somehow
my mom & my dad remembered
the mountains outside vienna

& they forgot
to hate certain last names
& then ted & my mom
were singing german lieder
i'd never heard

their harmony like feathered seeds
on the breeze.
& my mom laughed & said
i haven't thought of these songs
in forty years.

& my dad laughed
(with the sun making his eyes squinch up
& a tiny yellow butterfly floated past)
& i saw him reach out
to touch my mom's hand.

Stewart J. Florsheim

The Jewish Singles Event

Here are those who are challenged by,
it's hard to meet someone;
those who have taken to heart,
not only the importance of marriage,
but marriage to the right person.
We surround the dance floor, and,
just like in summer camp,
the men are on one side,
women on the other.
The band begins with a tune by the Stones.
A bold man, the one with the beard
and the Calvin Klein suit
who has no doubt considered law school, medical school,
and is now a photographer,
walks over to the woman in gold lamé shoes.
She seems so disinterested
that an earthquake would not startle her;
that the chandelier, falling from the ceiling,
would seem like an ocean of diamonds.

Moms and dads of the world,
look how hard we are trying.
Wasn't it easier forty years ago
when marriages were arranged,
and survival was the issue.
You watched lovers holding each other
through barbed wire fences,
and heard about the experiments
on the wombs of Jewish women.
You wanted us to have a better life,
so you have given us everything

that you could not have—
the finest clothing,
appliances that can spin, blend, chop, dice
the most wilted produce.
And a world where we can choose
what we want to do,
and whether or not we want to marry.
We haven't come a long way
to want to live alone, but it is easy;
only the ghosts are there:
their branded arms embrace us.

Stewart J. Florsheim

Business in Germany

1.
At the airport hotel,
my room is tiny
and smells as though
it has been sanitized
thousands of times—
the bleached sheets,
disinfected bathrooms.
In a drawer,
a German copy of Gideon's
is opened to Romans 12:9—
"Your love must be sincere.
Detest what is evil,
cling to what is good."
On the room service menu,
a big smiling face says,
"Get up on the right side:
Order breakfast NOW;"
inside, a listing of the meals
we had as kids—
Kalbsbraten, Wienerschnitzel,
Wurst, Sauerkraut.
I have a single bed
on a platform
made of fake rosewood
and on the small desk
that matches the bed—
a single unopened rose.

2
I turn on the T.V.—
a clip on the National Socialist Party
in the 1940's.
Hitler is marching down a street,
accompanied by his generals
and a brass band.
On another channel—
a news feature
about the rise in the sale of Mercedes.
I think about my parents
who say they would never buy
a German product.
They would also never return
to Germany,
not, they say, if their lives
depended on it.

3.
In "Die Zeit,"
an article about the new wave
of anti-Semitism—
a small village in the Austrian Alps
where the people's hatred goes back
to the days of Christ
who, they say, was murdered by Jews.
I hesitate,
then ask a young colleague
if this rise in anti-Semitism is true.
He says he doesn't know,
but they have only begun
to teach about World War II
in the schools,
and most people over 50
will not talk about the war at all.

4.
I begin to speak German
only to the people I think I can trust,
those from my generation—
a stewardess,
a parking garage attendant.
They see my copy of the English "Herald"
and appreciate the effort.
Others ask the question
about my accent—
it seems so authentic,
where did you get it?
One time I told an elderly concierge,
and she asked me if I like German beer,
and if the weather in the U.S.
is as cool as it is in Germany
this time of year.

5.
Back in my room,
the maid has turned back the quilt,
left a piece of Swiss chocolate
on my pillow.
In a dream,
I describe to my parents
an elaborate German dinner I had—
venison, home-made noodles,
wild mushrooms, lamb's lettuce.
They disapprove of the meal,
and wonder what I was doing
in Germany anyway.
I tell them
I was only there on business,
and no, I didn't speak German
to anyone.

Florence Wallach Freed

A Private School for Girls
May 14, 1948, New York City

The Headmaster addresses the Assembly
his words drip like poison into
my fifteen year old ears
"I don't see why the Jews need to
have their own country in Israel,
the Jews are supposed to be a
religion, not a nationality"
teachers lower their weary eyes
students bend over cramped notes
memorizing the French Revolution

No one ever argues with Mr. Dexter
a stately gentleman from Maryland
a silverhaired presence in his sixties
there are no Negroes in his school
except Dan and Sally who serve us
platters of ham, sweet potatoes, biscuits
but since the white Protestant families
have been moving to Darien, Connecticut
he's been forced to accept some
Jewish students into his private school

I see my saddle-shoes and bobby-sox
striding down the aisle toward the platform
I hear myself shouting, "The Jews are a religion
but the refugees from Hitler need a place to go"
my white middy blouse under my blue serge uniform
is drenched with sweat, I return to my seat
no one says a word, Assembly is dismissed
the quiz on the French Revolution is a snap
I write enthusiastically in my Blue Book
about the guillotining of Louis the Sixteenth

Sari Friedman

Answering Machine Message

Micki,
The message on your new machine
sounds lonely. What's going on?
You never call your old mother just because
she never calls you. How's Jason?
We're fine. No news.
The most exciting thing that's happened
I dreamed. I thought the Nazis
were coming to take away Laura.
I thought the Nazis were coming
to take away me. I woke
and stood in her doorway and watched
her sleep.
It's so easy to love her.
I love you too. I know
you don't believe me.
After nine months carrying you
I still couldn't believe
I had a baby. You don't know
what they did to babies then.
The clothes you were dressed in—
well I wore worse. How
can I explain?
Why do I try? It was better
for you to grow up unforgiving, independent.
It made you strong.
I loved you. You were my best,
my firstborn. The one
I really protected.
I let you go.
Call.

Sari Friedman

Skin

I
Mother, they say we never really leave you.
At the moment our bodies part,
a new mutual dependence arises.

But from the look of you,
the limp color and dissonant rattling,
angers inflaming you for brief wild moments
from inside,
it seems impossible that I ever started
from one as you, or existed alongside.

II
I wasn't meant to see
that time you tried to kill yourself,
but I did, and that small thing
saved you.
I dragged you back
like picking through garbage.
What was left of you
didn't want to exist.

III
When you fled from the Germans,
and the gooseflesh fear,
their teeth sinking through your creamy layers,
you even escaped from yourself, and arrived,
still burning inside like the ovens.

And you changed your name to Mary;
almost happy in a swirl of houses, clothes,
freckles, and a child . . .
the silly wet sponge, always crying.

IV
You tried to be a good mother,
but like everything else in your life,
it went wrong.
Breakfast after breakfast you piled
all the emptied eggshells back
into their original cartons,
and burnt all the eggs,
and became confused by our eyes.

If you were to read these words—
Would you understand? Would you see?
Would you collapse sobbing?
Freed?

V
Hey Ma does it hurt much?
You push back your hair,
palm up, a girlish gesture;
and a feel for the broken crunch of you,
the hurt of you,
my love a salve or a stab,
washes over, relentless.
What is left of you?

VI
I cannot know.
I am not you.
I am your American child
and I want my mother.
I still look for your face,
that skin I know so well,

love, even if I love alone.
In one face, the shadows of another.
In swells and hollows,
hope.

Barbara Goldberg

Our Father

God Himself, in all His righteous wrath
could not have been more terrifying
than when you raised your fist and thundered,
"Donnerwetter noch mal!"
Plates trembled, water spilled
and we froze, waiting for
your lightning hand to strike.

That ponderous daughter you admonished,
"Open your mouth, say something!"
now lectures groups of men about computers.
The younger girl you thought would have it
easy, the one you tried to toughen up,
today pays to be heard and weaves words
which do not support her in the style
to which she never grew accustomed.

True, we owe you our lives: paranoia's
useful in uncertain times. Hearing
distant troups, you forced Mother to flee
Czechoslovakia. How could you know
the shadows of those who died rose
at night to do their lone soft shoe?
And I, how could I know when I played
at your feet, you still heard boots.

Richard Michelson

The Queen Esther Award

... The criteria considered by the
celebrity judges are spiritual beauty
and commitment to a life of service.
The contestants will appear in
swimwear by Playboy. The winner will
receive the coveted Queen Esther
Award.
—Jewish Weekly News

How can I endure to see the evil that
shall come upon my kindred?
—Book of Esther

In the most inconceivable places,
Auschwitz for one, competitions were held
for the cleanest barracks. I can't stand clutter
to this day, my grandmother whispers,
although you'd think it would be the other way.

I shift in my seat. On stage
the evil Haman clowns and rages, confides
his plan of genocide, his hate
for Mordachai the Jew. The children boo
and shake their fists. Grandmother hisses
and stomps her feet. No one's afraid.
Behind me, the smell
of Purim cookies baking
for the party following the masquerade.

My daughter is Queen Esther for an hour.
At eight, she barely remembers her speeches
but knows she was chosen
for her beauty which, pleasing the King,
will save her people. Praying each line

108

we practiced stays with her,
I say the words to myself
but too loudly, like a man who has lived
too long without women.

We lined up and they looked us over.
Filth, they said, dogs, My head was shaved.
Celebrity judges—Mengele, Hoess.
If there were mirrors I'd have taken my life,
the lives of my children. Waved left
I was saved by no merit but chance.

My daughter runs towards me but girlfriends
engulf her. Laughing they lift the crown
from her head. Each tries it on, poses
for the others. I marvel at the beauty
of these young Jewish women
with their long braided hair, looking nothing
like the children of the children of survivors.

Richard Michelson

The Jews That We Are

> . . . you have inherited its burden
> without its mystery.
> —Elie Wiesel

I

March 1979 and I am watching Nazis
march through Chicago. The bold type
of the *Sun-Times* describes a small band
of hoodlums, undereducated boyscouts, the better
to be ignored. My grandfather, back
hunched over his Bible, agrees. Jews like myself
should stay home, should lay down
our stones and pray like the Jews that we are.

II

Grandfather, you are easy to love
with your long beard and the way you sway
like a palm branch in the storm. It is easy
to romanticize your spiritual search,
worldly naivete and wise rabbinical words.
You belong to the books I read
by Singer, Peretz, Sholom Aleichem.
But their characters are ignorant
of the chapters to come. You know
where their prayers will lead.

III

A circle. Six Nazis. Full military garb.
Your daughter naked in the middle. A gang-
rape and you're more ashamed than angry.
One soldier says all Jewesses are whores
and the others agree. You say nothing.

Years later you'll decide to speak:
"Do we not serve Hitler's purpose, we
who would sooner renounce our beliefs
than assume our burdens?" My mother
turns aside. Afraid
to answer. Silent even in her dreams.

IV
A generation after the Holocaust
and I know no Hebrew, no Torah. I fast
only on the day of atonement
and even then I've been known to cheat.
A generation after the Holocaust
and I apologize for my grandfather's
bent back and wild gestures.
I used to tremble to the discordant
rhythm of his prayers. I feared the mysterious
words that kept us from the devil.
Next to me my mother slept. She never cried
out in her dreams for his protection.
From her window she watches Nazis
march. Their feet strike the pavement
like the constant ticking of a clock.
I am a Jew a generation after the Holocaust.
Poorer, my grandfather says, without a past,
than he, who has no future.

Richard Michelson

Where I Sat

I sat between Grandmother
and Aunt Etta.
I never had a chance.

Grandmother would point to
her forearm, the numbers
tattooed there and that's
how I learned to count.
Aunt Etta told lies about
men who had loved her
when she was a young
coquette. I sat

like the silence
between train whistles
and dreamt

of the first woman
that took me to bed.
She was so beautiful
I never had a chance;
her skin
as smooth
as her silence. I heard
bells and sat
like a boy mid-bath,
between curiosity
and my own nakedness.

I sat between Grandmother
and Aunt Etta.

Between spoonfuls
of regret
they fed me
from this you shouldn't know
and may you never forget.

Gail Newman

Recording History

Out of the dark theatre into sunlight
so bright the air blurs. Prisms of light
shimmer on the sidewalk,
fall through branches of trees.

The tape recorder wouldn't record, the xerox machine
wouldn't copy, I locked my keys in the car.
The therapist taps his pencil on the desk:

> *Answer all the questions on the form.*

Stuck in mud, they throw you a rope. They want to pull
you out. Why aren't you *moving*?

      Moving, moving like the wheels on a car,
tires spinning. He nods his head and puts you in a box,
in his mind.

My mother was in a box, a cattle car, naked, moving through
the forest, when the tracks splintered, the bomb fell,
something flew through the door past her shoulder, blind,
like some invisible animal in the darkness.

He'd like to know how it feels. Flicks on the switch
of the tape recorder to take the words away
blind helpless mother want   If only he had been there.

Evelyn Posamentier

Counting Backwards

(1973)

you & your sisters said i had the head of a thirty year old.
at 6, i believed you, you were my mother,
& an orthodox jew doesn't lie; you said this
& i heard you, thru my tears as you
dragged me to the synagogue—
the unwanted dress squeezed tighter than a boa.

at 13, when my suicide face hung plain as the ironed
shirts that you folded away so neatly,
i asked
& you turned away,
i cried
& you snapped on the radio—
we always ate lunch quietly.

at 16,
when i exposed the nightly horror films that entered my life
without knocking, you said that i
thought too much
was influenced by the wrong crowd
didn't really have much to complain about considering
i didn't come from a broken home (or anything like that)

& besides, what did i think the young girls
did in dachau?

Evelyn Posamentier

The Bird Named Isidore

(in memory of my father,
Ernest Posamentier)

there is a story about a hummingbird named isidore.
in the story, also, is the man who owns him.
this is a children's story but adults, too, secretly
yearn for it.
the man & the bird isidore are seen against
the backdrop of a faraway city.
in the city there is a palace.
the palace appears
in each illustration.
silent symphonies are heard in blue orchestration
whenever the palace rises in the pink & weightless mind
of the reader.
the bird is white as a spot
of happiness in a fairy tale.
the bird named isidore watches from his window
as the man & his friends ride the ferris wheel.
& all the air hums with dreams.
because one of the pages is missing
& next we see the man in a dark factory
groping through a life in a language he doesn't
understand, we fear
that something terrible has happened.
sadly the pages turn.
over the years, love & light
dim to a steady drone.
but sometimes
in a bright yellow moment
of a sunday morning when the stores are closed
the bird stirs the wings in the man's mind, its breeze

116

sets slowly in motion the ferris wheel, the ferris wheel.
he mentions, half whispering, to his children
the story about the bird named isidore so near
to the touch.   one of the children waits
for more stories
but there are none:
the man has no past.
Only this one white spot.
the child is too frightened to ask:
& what else happened?

Lisa Ress

Household Rules. Farwell Avenue, Chicago, 1946

1
She turns onions into zeroes on the cutting board,
lines up the sheets at the edges of the linen cupboard shelves.
At four o'clock exactly she is marching X's with her needle
uniformed in thread along the borders of a tablecloth.
She shows me how to get up the stairs, how to come down,
how to lie in bed so no one can find me.
The knock on the door of this house in this country
is that of the milkman.
But I know I must ask myself
what is milk, what is coal, what do they mean
saying "Good morning, Lisa," as I cross the street.

2
She papers the kitchen with pictures of bodies
tangled like insects in ditches.
This could be you, she tells me.
I am a child, I say. I am not
supposed to know this, knowing anyway
that soon, or yesterday, I will be one of them, I am.
Drink your milk, she says, but it is white
elixir that will make me live too long.
At school the kids push me flat against the chain link fence.
How shall I keep them from knowing
how far it is all right for them to go?

Irene Reti

I Never Knew I Was Jewish

I.
My mother, born Jewish
in Nazi Germany
cannot remember her childhood,
even going to school,
except for fragments.

But she remembers
November ninth, 1938—
Kristallnacht.
She was eleven
lying in her room upstairs
in her tall brick house.
They broke into the houses of the Jews,
took many fathers away.
They did not take her father,
but wrecked every room except hers.
Her mother said,
"There's a little girl in there."

Kristallnacht—
I look for it in a book on the Holocaust.
I have read manifestos of lesbian liberation
to rooms of women, boldly,
carried gay books on crowded buses in strange cities:
but this history I absorb in a dark corner of the bookstore,
with furtive glances and cold hands.
Kristallnacht—
synagogues burnt
homes broken into rubble.
Seven and a half thousand

Jewish businesses destroyed in a single evening—
a rain of shattered plate glass.
One thousand
Jews murdered.
Twenty Six Thousand
deported to concentration camps.

But I want to know why, and how.
How did they get in the door?
Did they
dismember tables
burn feather beds
crush china
shred family portraits
steal money
rape women.
Whom did they take away   and why
and why not my grandfather?
It was not compassion.
Why did they leave my mother's room alone?
Was it something in the
set of my grandmother's face—
"There's a little girl in there."

It is 1985.
Tell me why
ninth graders draw swastikas across blackboards,
why a swastika is embedded
in the concrete of my neighborhood sidewalk;
who buys
genuine Nazi officer insignia
proudly sold at the antique store in San Francisco?

Tell me why immigration quotas for Jews
were set so low.
My mother's family was among few to escape.
She and her teenage sister

crossed the Atlantic alone on a steamer
through a submarine war zone
flotsam from sunken ships
dresses
dolls
chairs
floating mid-ocean.

My grandfather lost his toy factory
came to America, worked as a butler
my grandmother a seamstress
my aunt a punch press operator.
My mother, the "enemy alien" had to apply for a permit to go
to Girl Scout Camp, high school
dated boys in smart GI uniforms
tried to be an American girl,
felt ashamed of her immigrant parents
felt ashamed to feel ashamed of them.

II.
My father was also a Jewish refugee.
Yet they raised me
without Jewish history, without Jewish culture,
they hid it from me—
till at my grandfather's funeral
I asked, "What language are they speaking?"

Then I congratulated myself on not looking Jewish.
My red curls will protect me, I thought.
My blue eyes and white skin
give me amnesty.

Yet this was the same
frizzy hair and anemic complexion
they teased me about in school.
"Pale legs! Carrots!",
they taunted me.
They were straight, blond.

Sitting at dinner with my cousins
I insisted I didn't have a Jewish nose.
They laughed   bitterly.

In the schools of the 1970's
we watched films on the Holocaust,
studied the obligatory chapters
on black slavery, Indian village life,
the unit on the suffragettes.
We all read *The Diary of Anne Frank*
and sobbed into our pillows.

I remember feeling
bewildered, appalled by these stories.
But I was not Jewish;
I did not grieve or rage.
I shook my head sadly
as liberal white people do
over black unemployment
as sensitive men deplore
violence against women.

I did not grieve or rage.
I shook my head.
Now I hold my mother's
shattered memories in my fists.
How shall I use them?

Tell me
how shall I mourn?

My best friend and I eat brunch
at a deli filled with Jews.
She orders lox.
I stare at the bright pink strips, salty on her plate,
fascinated.
I tell her—

Kristallnacht.
Her blue eyes see directly through
my nervous smile.
She cries.
People stare.
She cries
but I stare mutely at my eggs.
Tell me
how shall I mourn?

III.
I am the woman with double vision.
I have been the sympathetic outsider
and the one whose parents survived the fire,
who cannot speak with pride of holidays, folklore,
whose Jewishness is mute,
who knows everything about silence
and nothing about dancing.

Jane Schapiro

The Tourist

Auschwitz, 1986

Hard to say why some of us have come this far
just to press against cold brick,
touch the metal of a wire fence.
Surely we've heard
the echoes of our heels before,
felt the crumble of dirt beneath our shoes,
the hardness of stone.
We've seen charred wood, rusted springs,
broken shutters,
listened to the creak of a swinging door.
Even these fields are old hand,
grass is grass,
it bends wherever a wind blows.

Here only the visible remains,
doorknobs, iron nails,
and us; the bones which rise again
and again. This time let's
not wonder about what has been or
will be. Just once
let us try the other way where
the body leads,
where cells replenish when given the chance,
mothers live to feed their young.

Dora Weeks

When I was ten
I used to wonder
What my family had done
Why they had put
My uncles and my aunts in ovens
Cousins too, little ones,
One was seven when he died
Three years before I was born
So I grew up an only child
No brothers sisters uncles cousins
One aunt who spent the war hiding in Brussels
She sang me a lullaby: "you're a good not good not good"
She would never have dinner with us
My mother kept confessing to the police to a murder she hadn't done
She could not understand why she had been allowed to live when
        most all of her family had died.
My father was different, raised from nine in America
He told me that it was not true, the grown-ups had been talking about
        something else, nobody was killed, the camps were so they
        would work
His intentions were good
To shield me from the truth
But I only learned to mistrust him
And keep close to my mother
Who kept repeating her twisted tales of murders
And shadows that were a sign that they were out to get her.
When I was ten
I used to wonder
When I was 20 and 30 I forgot
When I was 38,
I began to remember
And began to forgive my family for its craziness

And myself for my craziness
When I was ten
I used to wonder
What my family had done.

V

Rain of the Blue Tattoos

Marvin Bell

The Extermination of the Jews

A thousand years from now
they will be remembered as heroes.
A thousand years from now
they will still be promised their past.

Objects of beauty notwithstanding,
once more they will appear
for their ruin, seeking a purse,
hard bread or a heavy weapon

for those who must survive,
but no one shall survive.
We who have not forgotten,
our children shall outremember:

their victims' pious chanting—
last wishes, last Yiddish, last dreaming—
were defeats with which the Gestapo
continues ceasing and ceasing.

Marvin Bell

Getting Lost in Nazi Germany

You do not move about, but try
to maintain your position. Would you eat
the fruit of the corpses?—You would.
Your friends are the points of a star
now a golden, unattainable "elsewhere"
because there is no elsewhere for a Jew.

Men have closed their daughters to you,
and now the borders like neat hairlines
limiting your ideas to hatred and escape.
This way, they have already begun
the experiments with your brain—
later to be quartered and posted.

Cremations of what remains?
In a dream like this one, a weathered face
will drive you off under a load of hay
at the very moment the Commandant calls.
You could swear the voice you hear is kind,
calling you home, little Jewboy in alarm.

Joseph Glazer

Drinking with the Nazis

Down the street their script on every window!
In Basel on the Rhine all we had to do was
Walk a little faster, and
Beer-gardens with oom-pa-pas came out
To tease you.

A hall full of tables, chairs, and
Shadows peopled, women like shot-putters from
Russia in the Olympics,
One could have been cousin Hilda Lubliner
Who told me she had run many hurdles.

These figures, mothers, fathers, kin
Worked right through it . . .
How could I drink with them then?

Well, that band! The jumpiest trio in
Switzerland, rollicking, frolicking,
Bellowing, "Come now, come on."

The service prompt and courteous,
Not Frenchified, friendly
Sans scorn.

And, natürlich, steins foaming lager which
With us imported, localized there,
Surpassed nectar.

Two women in a corner waltzed together—
Mama hopped about like that at weddings—
I asked myself: Forgive? Forget? Does it matter?

131

(Over and over, crests and troughs,
Love and hate, hot and cold,
Oh, rid me of it all . . .)

Our waiter must have heard, brought another stein-full,
Suddenly the pall lifted,
Up, up, with the alcohol.

William Heyen

The Numinous

> Our language has no term that can
> isolate distinctly and gather into one
> word the total numinous impression a
> thing may make on the mind.
> —Rudolf Otto

We are walking on a sidewalk
in a German city.
We are watching gray smoke
gutter along the roofs
just as it must have
from other terrible chimneys.
We are walking our way
almost into a trance.
We are walking our way
almost into a dream
only those with blue
numbers along their wrists
can truly imagine.

Now, just in front of us, something
bursts into the air.
For a few moments
our bodies echo fear.
Pigeons, we say,
only an explosion
of beautiful blue-gray pigeons.
Only pigeons that gather
over the buildings
and begin to circle.

We are walking again, counting
all the red poinsettias

between the windowpanes
and lace curtains.
It was only
a flock of pigeons:
we can still see them
circling over the block buildings,
a hundred hearts
beating in the air.
Beautiful blue-gray pigeons.
We will always remember.

David Lampert

Poem for Sophie

it is simply this
at the end, as was fit
i found a girl, age three or four
who was the most in need
she kept calling for mommy
and i held her
until she slept, woke, and slept again
we played a game
and otherwise did not listen
we sang
it was possible
for a short time
and again

(here
a sea otter
appears
a cormorant, starting low
touching the water
a pelican, just above the wave
no wing movement
flying straight
another coming to a rock
coming in slow
several birds on the sea
sunrise
the cormorant
beating its wings very hard)

she said "my mommy chose to leave me"
in a very fine polish

i asked her how
and she said how
and in due course
rocks back to the sea
we slept
they turned on the gas, at auschwitz
she and i were at a soft hum
flying low

Lyn Lifshin

Hearing of Reagan's Trip to Bitburg

as maples turn the size
of babies' hands   the
last thing mothers
saw as the screaming
wriggling bodies were
thrown into fires   hands
buried above some grave
as if waving goodby
or pulling you with
them. Suddenly I'm in
the yellow room   color
of new willows, sun
tulips   the daffodils
breaking down   woke
up each night dreaming
of tunnels and fire,
the words whispered in
front of the apart
ment, rain of the
blue tattoos. The gas,
words like cattle cars
changed as the word
camp   so when I went
to Camp Hochelega   I
waited for gas, held
my breath   couldn't
sleep with lights off.

Christopher Millis

The IRT at Rush Hour

They must have died like this at Auschwitz,
crowded and thoughtless,
sweat sealing their clothes.

They must have looked at one another
when the intercom garbled its instructions
and the weak ones slumped into laps.

They must have imagined their stop,
how they would disembark underground
into the cool station.

Gail Newman

An Anti-Semitic Demonstration

from a photograph by Roman Vishniac

There are hundreds of people in the street.
This could be New York or Chicago.
Traffic is stopped in the cold.
The men are bare-headed, wearing long
heavy coats, and some of them are running
with raised arms, their flat palms lifted
like white slashes against the sky. The dark
bodies move in formation across that ordinary
street, a street with lamp posts and gutters,
a street with automobiles and drug stores and stains
that could be the scuff marks of hundreds of shoes
marching, or car oil, or blood.
The faces of the crowd are far away and small
with features indistinct as smudged charcoal.
I don't know the name of this street,
but I know it is Poland, 1938, and my mother
may be living close by, listening at the window
with the shades drawn, listening to the future
rushing toward her like a wave, listening to her heart
beat against her sixteen year old breast like a finger
tapping on glass.
I'd like to push this crowd back along the narrow
littered street, back into the past
when my mother's arm was still bare, before
a blue number was branded there.

Karen Propp

Train Passage

Not the train my grandfather escaped
by taking the last boat to America.
Not that train. No, when
he saw women scrub the streets of Vienna,
he packed the family into a furniture truck,
and crossed the border. Two years
hidden in Brussels: my mother at the convent school
in the long curls my grandmother continued to twist
as if they would still stroll in the park,
visit friends, and attend concerts;
the curls my mother tossed and flung
at the gendarme who'd seized my grandfather,
told him he'd be going away
on a little journey, and yes, if she wanted to,
my grandmother could pack some sandwiches.
That afternoon in the bureau
everything was reduced: my mother
weeping, holding fast to my grandfather,
my grandmother quieting the baby,
the officer's trim uniform and a face
he'd barely begun to shave.
That afternoon, everything was reduced
to the gendarme's word: *Allez!*
And his singular turning
so the family could see his back.
Before the officer could turn again,
my grandfather, very pale and threadbare,
took my mother's hand
into the bright and dusty street.

Not the Bronx to Brooklyn train
my grandfather rode
with his plain-faced alarm clock
in his coat pocket. He slept and set
the alarm to ring at the station,
or read the *New York Times*, every word,
and the sports page twice.
Thirty years in the factory
directing the assembly of dolls
from the heap of flawless limbs and torsos;
regal dolls who stared with glassy eyes
and black lashes on my birthday mornings.
Not even the train I took across America to see
the states that belonged to their names,
the fields and farms and fields
where one or two lights blinked.
Never again, people say, and I think
of my grandfather's grave voice
searching for a way to speak.

Anne Ranasinghe

Auschwitz from Colombo

Colombo, March. The city white fire
That pours through vehement trees burst into flame
And only a faint but searing wind
Stirring the dust
From relics of foreign invaders, thrown
On this far littoral by chance or greed,
Their stray memorial the odd word mispronounced,
A book of laws
A pile of stones
Or maybe some vile deed.

Once there was another city; but there
It was cold—the trees leafless
And already thin ice on the lake.
It was that winter
Snow hard upon the early morning street
And frost flowers carved in hostile window panes—

It was that winter.

Yet only yesterday
Half a world away and twenty-five years later
I learn of the narrow corridor
And at the end a hole, four feet by four,
Through which they pushed them all—the children too—
Straight down a shaft of steel thirteen feet long
And dark and icy cold
Onto the concrete floor of what they called
The strangling room. Dear God, the strangling room,
Where they were stunned—the children too—
By heavy wooden mallets,

Garroted, and then impaled
On pointed iron hooks.

I am glad of the unechoing street
Burnt white in the heat of many tropical years.
For the mind, no longer sharp,
Seared by the tropical sun
Skims over the surface of things
Like the wind
That stirs but slightly the ancient dust.

Anne Ranasinghe

Sinhala New Year 1975

The morning of Sinhala New Year I went to the market
To buy mangoes, a pineapple and kolikuttu
Plaintains.   A lorry drove up

Four men jumped down from the lorry, loosened the chains,
The tail-gate fell, and inside the lorry
Lay the little pink bodies

Of skinned goats and their babies, also skinned and shiny
Pink, so many of them, naked, hairless and without heads,
The stumps of their delicate necks

Still oozing blood.   The men
Heaved them up on their shoulders, in twos and in threes,
And carried them quickly to the stall

Where already the chickens were hanging, neatly in rows,
Also skinned, and without heads, suspended
From a piece of string.

For the goats however they had hooks which pierce sharply
Through the tender part between the hindlegs.
The men worked fast and

Very precisely, and though I averted my eyes
From the fixed stare of those skinless bodies
Their voiceless bleating

Pierced the mind,   which remembered
Other lorries and other bodies on meathooks—
Not under a tropical sun, but

144

In the knife-sharp cold of a cemented cellar. A
Silly comparison, I told myself, pull yourself together
And wish the butcher a Happy New Year.

Lisa Ress

Learning the Ropes. Custer Street. Evanston, 1949

Showering, I see more than the single showerhead,
and test myself, how long I can go without breathing.
The icy road to school is my grandparents' way to work camp.
I make it through.
The elevated is a cattle car that seals me in with strangers.
I study them. Who will be the first to crack?
Who will not look away when I have to go to the bathroom?

Sundays before our parents awake, my sister and I jump our wrecked
        ship,
hit the refrigerator for provisions to stock our beds.
We rescue each stuffed animal.
This time we will get away with our lives.

Lisa Ress

The Visit, Auschwitz, 1971

Dr. Bronowski stands in the marshes.
He has come back to Poland and squats in hard shoes,
scooping silt and pouring it hand to hand.
Here, says Dr. Bronowski, his glances
concentrating light,
are the ashes of four million people.
We watch the thin mud of our parents
slip through his hands.

He speaks to us wading. The wetness
climbs in his shoes. At the viscid center
the sky has become his eyes, the pond skin
folds itself against him, hugging his flesh.

David Shevin

What He Hated

> Why, he hated the Germans. He
> always spoke very unfavorably about
> them. He's as fine an American as you
> would want to have next door.
> —Milton Hendricks, quoted in the
> *Cincinnati Post* on learning that his
> neighbor, Leonid Petkiewytch, was a
> Gestapo guard convicted at
> Nuremburg of war crimes.

What he hated was the blood in the corner of the eye
of an adolescent's lost and desperate stare,
like the eye of a trout floundering on a hot rock.
What he hated was the way that the poplars
past the fence at Kiel-Hasse would not stop singing
with the legs of crickets mating or twigs
snapping beneath the animals like the tiny
bones in the human ear. And he hated the breath
of the dying old, like a candle trying to sputter
in the thin, bitter atmosphere of the moon.
And the mud near the men's gymnasium that spit
to his cuffs where it grabbed like a menace
begging heed. In the summer he hated the starch
of his uniform, cloth biting as though to be one
with his skin. In winter he hated the curses and gossip
of the dead in the telephone lines of the wind.

He was good to the children, the neighbors said.
And he brought tomatoes from the rich river soil
in the yard, and flowers from the garden. He kept
to himself and was kind when he spoke. You could not ask
for a finer—

What he hated was how the migration of train cars
now empty would jolt him from sleep. And he hated
the drum of a stick on a ribcage like the irregular march
of battalions of cripples. And the way the truck motors
would cough out in hunger while night cold came clawing
through cracked wooden slats. And the way
the low roof on the showers would cut a short horizon
where last month's souls would climb out.

And a fat raccoon was waking in the cold Ohio night.
The fur on his neck shone fine as spun glass.

Nancy Shiffrin

Anna's Dream

Ovens. Women in line waiting for showers.
With mutilated wombs. With monsters implanted.
Some refused to be prostitutes. The old woman
she fed and bathed gives her a baby's trusting smile.

Suddenly a thousand women queue up behind her stove.
The bread they bake does not rise. Yeasty dough
leaks out. They stick together in it.

She wakes chilled, sweaty, pulls at damp clothes.
Daughter bursts in, "Mommy, I'm hungry."
She goes to the kitchen, turns on the gas.
Her hands shake. She cannot strike the match.
Then—smell of sulphur. Explosion.

Screaming child.
Solace of singed eyebrows.

Alina Tugend

Every Few Months

Every few months
I dream of Nazis
Escaping, terrified
vainly leaping out of windows, climbing through tunnels
Once in a while
I am not a Jew
but desperately hiding others
I always awake with tangled sheets
look at the Washington trees outside
and think of Germany

I learned of Nazis
from the day I was born
Evil incarnate
it has not dimmed
Orthodox Jews have God
as their one absolute
We have the Nazis

I saw Auschwitz in Poland
piles of shoes and eyeglasses
it has not dimmed

During the day
there are real life fears
unfinished stories, unpaid bills, unfulfilled loves
but at night
there are the Nazis

C. K. Williams

A Day for Anne Frank

> God hates you!
> —St. John Chrysostom

1.

I look onto an alley here
where, though tough weeds and flowers thrust up
through cracks and strain
toward the dulled sunlight,
there is the usual filth spilling from cans,
the heavy soot shifting in the gutters.
People come by mostly
to walk their dogs or take the shortcut
between the roaring main streets,
or just to walk
and stare up at the smoky windows,
but this morning when I looked out
children were there running back and forth
between the houses toward me.
They were playing with turtles—
skimming them down the street
like pennies or flat stones,
and bolting, shouting, after the broken corpses.
One had a harmonica, and as he ran,
his cheeks bloating and collapsing like a heart,
I could hear its bleat, and then the girls' screams
suspended behind them with their hair,
and all of them: their hard, young breath,
their feet pounding wildly on the pavement to the corner.

2.

I thought of you at that age.
Little Sister, I thought of you,

152

thin as a door,
and of how your thighs would have swelled
and softened like cake,
your breasts have bleached
and the new hair growing on you like song
would have stiffened and gone dark.
There was rain for a while, and then not.
Because no one came, I slept again,
and dreamed that you were here with me,
snarled on me like wire,
tangled so closely to me that we were vines
or underbrush together,
or hands clenched.

3.
They are cutting babies in half on bets.
The beautiful sergeant has enough money to drink
for a week.
The beautiful lieutenant can't stop betting.
The little boy whimpers
he'll be good.
The beautiful cook is gathering up meat
for the dogs.
The beautiful dogs
love it all.
Their flanks glisten.
They curl up in their warm kennels
and breathe.
They breathe.

4.
Little Sister,
you are a clot
in the snow,
blackened,
a chunk of phlegm
or puke

and there are men with faces
leaning over you with watercans

watering you!
in the snow, as though flowers would sprout
from your armpits
and genitals.

Little Sister,
I am afraid of the flowers sprouting from you

I am afraid of the silver petals
that crackle
of the stems darting
in the wind
of the roots

5.
The twilight rots.
Over the greasy bridges and factories,
it dissolves
and the clouds swamp in its rose
to nothing.
I think sometimes the slag heaps by the river
should be bodies
and that the pods of moral terror
men make of their flesh should split
and foam their cold, sterile seeds into the tides
like snow
or ash.

6.
Stacks of hair were there
little mountains
the gestapo children must have played in
and made love in and loved
the way children love haystacks or mountains

O God the stink
of hair oil and dandruff

their mothers must have thrown them into their tubs
like puppies and sent them to bed

coming home so filthy stinking

of jew's hair

of gold fillings, of eyelids

7.
Under me on a roof
a sparrow little by little
is being blown away.
A cage of bone is left,
part of its wings,
a stain.

8.
And in Germany the streetcar conductors go to work
in their stiff hats,
depositing workers and housewives
where they belong,
pulling the bell chains,
moving drive levers forward or back.

9.
I am saying good-bye to you before our death. Dear
Father: I am saying good-bye to you before my death.
We are so anxious to live, but all is lost—we are not
allowed! I am so afraid of this death, because little
children are thrown into graves alive. Good-bye
forever.

I kiss you.

10.
Come with me Anne.
Come,
it is rotten not to be anywhere at all,
to have no one
like an old whore,
a general.

Come sit with me here
kiss me; my heart too is wounded
with forgiveness.

There is an end now.
Stay.
Your foot hooked through mine
your hand against my hand
your hip touching me lightly

it will end now
it will not begin again

Stay
they will pass
and not know us

the cold brute earth
is asleep

there is no danger

there is nothing

Anne

there is nothing

VI

We Are the Raging Fire

Talia N. Bloch

While Bouncing the Shema
Back and Forth in Shul

1
We were there, Avinu,
        when a mortal gift
        of flesh sealed the Covenant
        with Your Chosen Ones.
And so were You.

2
We were there, E-lohenu,
        when an angel's embrace
        blessed Your First Born
        with the name, Israel.
And so were You.

3
We were there, Moshienu,
        when the sole might
        of Your outstretched hand guided
        Your beloved Children
        from the chains of Pharaoh's
        bondage.
And so were You.

4

We were there, Malkenu,
      when Judaic shout
      of trumpets claimed
      a Homeland for Your Nation.
And so were You.

5

We were there, HaRachaman,
      when the winds of Your
      forgiveness
      swept us from our tears
      in Babylon to our laughter
      in Jerusalem.
And so were You.

6

We were there, A-do-nai,
      when the glory of Your Defenders
      shone for eight days
      with the purity of One.
And so were You.

7

We were there, G'd,
      when the life of Your Holy People
      was silently diffused
      into gas
      and their spirits chased
      into ovens.
And where were You?

("Uva-yom hashevii shabbat
      va-yinafash?")

Susan Dambroff

Resistance

I am built of my thoughts
I carefully arrange
and rearrange them

Impatient with old words
the ones that come so easily
assuming their place
in a sentence
like placemats

      It's something about my mind
           how it seems
           it is the one thing
      It's my room
      my house
      my country
           that can never
           be taken
   away

             • • •

I begin to eat books.
I know there is something I haven't been told.

I read:

"The question is not why did all the Jews not fight, but how so many
of them did."

"In practically every ghetto and in every labor and concentration camp there existed a Jewish underground organization that kept up the prisoners' morale, reduced their physical sufferings, committed acts of sabotage, organized escapes, collected arms, planned revolts, and, in many instances, carried them out."

I read partisans; I read heroes; I read heroines:

"It was Rosa Robota's secret smuggling apparatus that provided the dynamite used to blow up an Auschwitz crematorium."

As a runner and interpreter, Mala Zimetbaum "found a way to save the lives of hundreds of women prisoners."

Niuta Teitelboim was a "Jewish girl from the Warsaw Ghetto, whose underground name was "Wanda." . . . Though she operated mainly in the Warsaw area, Wanda became a legendary name throughout Poland, a symbol of fearless resistance to the German occupation forces."*

• • •

There were those
who escaped to the forests
who crawled through sewers
who jumped from the backs of trains

There were those
who smuggled messages
who smuggled dynamite
inside breadloaves
inside matchboxes
inside corpses

There were those
who were shoemakers

*Quotes from Yuri Suhl's *They Fought Back* (New York: Shocken Books, 1975).

who put nails
into the boots
of the German soldiers

There were those
who wrote poetry
who put on plays
who taught the children

There were those
who fed each other

And resistance
  was a bullet
    was a flame
      was singing
        was imagining
  was continuing to breathe
        • • •

I am in the bathtub. I have lit a blue candle.
The warm water eases my hectic day out of me.

Something swims in.
A name.
        Mala
            the way the sound
            softens the tongue
        Behind her . . .
        Wanda
            strong heat
            inside my jaw
        Like a bird out of water . . .
        Rosa
            comes in

Through the flame
they come
their fingers
up my back
into my throat
where they are singing
washing their stories
through my pores
and calling me

     I call
       them
     they call back
       back
       Back to back
     we call
       through the candle
       through the water
     we call
     the names roll out of my voice over and into each other
       Mala
          Rosa
            Wanda
     Rosa
            Rosa
       Mala   Wanda
            Mala
            Wanda

It is a shower
   our singing
our voices run down hills

Our hands are fighting and eating and passing and smuggling and
        scrubbing
and scratching and giving and taking and touching and holding on

And the singing is their courage moving into me.

Charles Fishman

Not Only in the Six-Day War

but in the locked ghettos
there were heroes,
in the selections, the cattle trains,
the forced marches, even under torture,
as the gas embraced them, in the smoke
billowing, in the blood ditches,
even in the death sleep after liberation,
the DP camps, the frail ships, desert
massacres, even in hospitals and orchards,
kibbutz nurseries, zealots' outposts,
even in the day-to-day dream of remembering
what was ours, over thousands of years,
in this moment when I remind you
my sisters and brothers, how courageous
we have been, how bravely
we have arrived at this hour.

William Heyen

To the Onlookers

(after Nelly Sachs)

When our backs are turned,
when someone stares at us,
we feel them.
You who watched the killing, and did nothing,
still feel the eyes of those dead
on your bodies.

How many see you
as you pick a violet?
How many oak branches twist
into hands begging for help?
How many memories congeal
in the sun's evening blood?

O the unsung cradlesongs
in the dove's nightcries—
so many would have loved
their own stars in the night skies,
but now only the old well
can do it for them.

You did not murder,
but looked on, you,
who could have been changed
into light.

Phyllis Kahaney

Germany, 1981

Berlin

Once in Berlin I rode
the subway all day,
scanned each old face
in that train as if
I could tell by looking
they were Nazis.
It was 1970—twenty-nine
years since they burned
my aunt alive. This
was my vendetta:
that day in the U-Bahn
I tracked down twelve
of them, named them,
sentenced them, imagined
them dead. At the exits
they stumbled out,
ghosts of themselves.

Ulm

His arms are pocked
with scars from
dug-out shrapnel.
His shoulders stoop
from the weight of epaulets
that now lie hidden
in his closet. He cleans
the ladies room in Ulm,
eyes blazing like the coins

he slides off the table.
He stares at the women
in mirrors. They brush
their hair, apply mascara
as if he were not there.

Ravensbrück

If Grandfather had stayed
in Karenetz and worked
his father's mill
I would be dead now,
or else alive in some hell
where salvation is not
to see men thin as snakes
dig grave after grave
and not be able themselves
to die. I would
go numb—my body
would become a shell
for its own ashes.

Heidenheim

In the valley three deer
cross a meadow. People
mill as people do
in the country after church.
Women carry picnics,
children ride their bikes,
men load cameras under trees.
You could forget. The sun
beats down on grandfathers
and children. They take hands
as the deer drift
toward the forest
no longer afraid.

Stuttgart

In Stuttgart they are
digging up the flowers.
It is May and the tulips
have been splendid; now
they lie in heaps wilting
in the morning drizzle.
Why I ask a workman
but he knows no English.
Why I ask a woman
crossing the road
but she shrugs.
Why I ask a businessman.
on his way to work
and I can see he knows
but the answer will not
form itself in words.

Rachel Loden

Conversations with Dr. M

They say it is you
at the morgue
in São Paulo:

skull, bones,
shreds of cloth;

they say they will know you
even from one tooth.

At the grave
they paraded your skull
for the curious,

tossed the remains
into a bin,
mangled evidence.

There are complaints.
But we of infinite patience
have endured

your many disinterments
in this world,
all of them careless.

Your dental records
have arrived in Brazil;
felicitations.

In a cold room
they count
and clean your bones,

assemble your skeleton,
match abnormality
with recorded injury.

They want to know
if you drowned;
we want to know

what images
possessed you
on the way down.

Herr Doktor,
is it you?

We of infinite patience
whose wounds
were never catalogued,

whose bones
were never counted,
want to know.

Seymour Mayne

In Memory of Aaron, Murdered Grandfather

He who shot my maternal grandfather, Aaron,
down on the road to the ghetto
is probably a grandfather himself now
retired on a good pension
in a prosperous hamlet of Bavaria

He drinks beer at the pub
each evening and belches
from potato salad and *Schnitzel*
Schwartzwaldtorte is his delight
and his grandchildren, clean, blond,
growing up without a tremor

Skullbones, killing you
would not be nearly enough
Perhaps eradicating
that legion of yours
and its teutonic stolidity
would be a start

Were your *Vaterland*
razed to the ground
it would not balance out
Even if it became an obscure
encyclopedia entry (Beethoven,
a passing mention)
filling in where the abscessed
pit of Europe rots
and an imperial race molds
into the dank soil
that spawned, spewed it forth
to stench the earth
as history's foulest footnote

Richard Michelson

Genuine Jewish Flesh

I

Rabbi Abe Rosen	returned
home from Hell	pulls from his pocket
a cake of soap.	Says, "Hope"
from his pulpit	"stinks
like an armpit.	Its smell
must be always	upon you."

II

White, she was, as mayonnaise on white bread
when Abe's smooth cheeked son cut his strings
and tied himself a tight goyisha knot.
"Milk" he said, "flows like life through her veins."
But then he sucked at her breast
and blood spilled like wine from a broken jar.
Never sleep with a Jew during times of war.

III

These things did happen
                    confessed the chaplain
who blessed the knife
                    that butchered Abe's wife.
This is the vat
                    where they boiled her fat
until it was soap.
                    This is the soap.

IV

Rabbi Abe Rosen   returned
home to Heaven   pulls from his pocket
a cake of soap.   Says, "Hope"
from his coffin   "hangs loose
like a foreskin.   Its weight
serves no purpose   to speak of."

Amos Neufeld

Children of Night

(for Elie Wiesel)

We live in this world
as though it had not
abandoned us, yet remember
the darkness as though it were today.
As though we ourselves
were the remnants
of the world we lost:
brothers and sisters to night,
the light of lost suns and moons,
the dust of dead stars.

We live in the aftermath, yet burn,
searching the earth and sky,
the ashes and dust,
for the burnt stars, the lost worlds,
the night from which we came.

We are the raging fire
that would have its revenge.
We would burn this world,
avenge our pain
were it not this late
here, now, in this different darkness,
yet always, closer to that night
to which, for us, there is no return.

C. K. Williams

Spit

> . . . then the son of the "superior race"
> began to spit into the Rabbi's mouth so
> that the Rabbi could continue to spit
> on the Torah. . . .
> —The Black Book

After this much time, it's still impossible. The SS man with his stiff
        hair and his uniform;
the Rabbi, probably in a torn overcoat, probably with a stained beard
        the other would be clutching;
the Torah, God's word, on the altar, the letters blurring under the
        blended phlegm;
the Rabbi's parched mouth, the SS man perfectly absorbed, obsessed
        with perfect humiliation.
So many years and what is there to say still about the soldiers waiting
        impatiently in the snow,
about the one stamping his feet, thinking, "Kill him! Get it over with!"
while back there the lips of the Rabbi and the other would have
        brushed
and if time had stopped you would have thought they were lovers,
so lightly kissing, the sharp, luger hand under the dear chin,
the eyes furled slightly and then when it started again the eyelashes of
        both of them
shyly fluttering as wonderfully as the pulse of a baby.
Maybe we don't have to speak of it at all, it's still the same.
War, that happens and stops happening but is always somehow right
        there, twisting and hardening us;
then what we make of God—words, spit, degradation, murder, shame;
        every conceivable torment.
All these ways to live that have something to do with how we live
and that we're almost ashamed to use as metaphors for what goes on
        in us

but that we do anyway, so that love is battle and we watch ourselves
in love
become maddened with pride and incompletion, and God is what it is
when we're alone
wrestling with solitude and everything speaking in our souls turns
against us like His fury
and just facing another person, there is so much terror and hatred that
yes,
spitting in someone's mouth, trying to make him defile his own
meaning,
would signify the struggle to survive each other and what we'll enact
to accomplish it.

There's another legend.
It's about Moses, that when they first brought him as a child before
Pharaoh,
the king tested him by putting a diamond and a live coal in front of
him
and Moses picked up the red ember and popped it into his mouth
so for the rest of his life he was tongue-tied and Aaron had to speak
for him.
What must his scarred tongue have felt like in his mouth?
It must have been like always carrying something there that weighed
too much,
something leathery and dead whose greatest gravity was to loll out
like an ox's,
and when it moved, it must have been like a thick embryo slowly
coming alive,
butting itself against the inner sides of his teeth and cheeks.
And when God burned in the bush, how could he not cleave to him?
How could he not know that all of us were on fire and that every word
we said would burn forever,
in pain, unquenchably, and that God knew it, too, and would say
nothing Himself ever again beyond this,
ever, but would only live in the flesh that we use like firewood,
in all the caves of the body, the gut cave, the speech cave:

He would slobber and howl like something just barely a man that
       beats itself again and again onto the dark,
moist walls away from the light, away from whatever would be light
       for this last eternity.
"Now therefore go," He said, "and I will be with thy mouth."

Biographies

KAREN ALKALAY-GUT teaches American literature at the University of Tel Aviv. Her third volume of poetry, *Mechitza*, was published in 1986 by Cross Cultural Communications. She is the founder of the Israel Association for Writers in English, and in 1984 was awarded the Arie Dulchin Prize for Literature from the Jewish Agency. She was born in London during the last night of the Blitz and emigrated to America with her family in 1948. Her Lithuanian parents had fled Danzig for England on the night of Hitler's invasion, after several failed attempts to reach "safe" countries like Palestine and Sweden. They spent the war years during the bombing of London attempting to obtain the release of other Jews from German-occupied areas.

MARVIN BELL is the author of eight books of poetry, a collection of essays, and (with William Stafford) two volumes of poems written as correspondence. Atheneum published his *New and Selected Poems* in 1987. He has been awarded The Lamont Award of the Academy of American Poets, Guggenheim and NEA Fellowships, and Senior Fulbright Appointments to Yugoslavia and Australia. He teaches for The University of Iowa, where he is Flannery O'Connor Professor of Letters, and lives part of each year in Port Townsend, Washington. His grandparents came from Russia, fleeing the pogroms of the Czar and the anti-Semitic violence of the Bolsheviks.

STEPHEN BERG is the author of *The Daughters* and *Grief: Poems and Versions of Poems* and is a founding editor of the *American Poetry Review*. He has also written *Nothing in the Word*, poems from the Aztec, and is a cotranslator of the volume *Clouded Sky*, poems of the Hungarian poet Miklos Radnoti. He was awarded the Frank O'Hara Memorial Prize in 1971 and a Guggenheim Fellowship in Poetry in 1974. He cotranslated *Oedipus the King* with Dishkin Clay. His book of poems, *With Akhmatova at the Black Gates*, was published in 1980. He teaches at the Philadelphia College of Art and Princeton University.

TALIA N. BLOCH is currently a student at Yale University, where she is pursuing a B.A. in comparative literature. Her father was born in Munich in 1928; his father spent six weeks in Dachau following Kristallnacht. In 1939, the Bloch family emigrated to the United States. Bloch's mother was born in Strasbourg, France, in 1934; she and her family emigrated to Israel in 1935.

BONNILEE is a poet residing in New Mexico. Her grandmother was forced away from her homeland in Russo-Poland as the pogroms became increasingly oppressive. She fled to America with her sister in 1920. Her mother and brothers did not follow; it is believed they perished in the Holocaust.

SUSAN DAMBROFF is a special education teacher in San Francisco, working primarily with autistic and emotionally disturbed children. Her first book of poetry, *Memory in Bone*, was published by Black Oyster Press in 1984. She grew up surrounded by images of the Holocaust. "My personal journey has led me to experience my internalized fear and then to move from that to a place of resistance and courage."

JOAN (THALER) DOBBIE lives in Eugene, Oregon, with her two children, where she is pursuing an M.F.A. in creative writing. Her poems have been published in various magazines and anthologies, and she self-published a chapbook of her own poetry titled *A Trip through Mama Kali's Zoological Garden*. She was born in Trogen, Switzerland, in 1946. Her parents fled there from Austria in 1938; the family then moved to the United States in 1948.

CHERYL J. FISH is a poet and fiction writer who lives in New York City. Her most recent poetry chapbook is *My City Flies By* (E.G. Chapbook Series, San Francisco) and her fiction has appeared in *Dreamworks* and *Between C&D*. She teaches at Brooklyn College and Rutgers University. Her grandmother was the sole survivor of a large family from Przemysalamy in Poland. As the eldest daughter, she emigrated to New York to live with her aunt when she was sixteen; years later, her entire family was killed by the Nazis.

CHARLES FISHMAN is a poet and director of programs in the arts at the State University of New York College of Technology at Farmingdale. He is the author of four books of poems, including *The Death Mazurka* (Timberline Press), an original book of poetry on the Holocaust. He also edited an anthology of poetry titled *Blood to Remember: American Poets on the Holocaust*. His grandfather and other members of his family emigrated to the United States from Poland in 1907. His uncle was killed by American Nazi bundists in Cortland, New York, in 1935.

STEWART J. FLORSHEIM is a poet who lives in San Francisco and grew up in the Washington Heights section of New York City. His poetry and translations have been widely published. Both of his parents are from Germany. His maternal grandfather spent six weeks in Dachau following Kristallnacht; he was released after his wife procured a visa for the family to move to the United States in 1939. Florsheim's father emigrated to the United States in 1934. Several members of both families perished in the Holocaust.

FLORENCE WALLACH FREED's poetry has been widely published in the United States. Throughout her childhood, she was aware that her parents' relatives were being exterminated in Warsaw and Minsk. Her husband is a Hungarian Jew who survived the Holocaust; he spent three years in Stalin's labor camps, and his mother and many other relatives were killed in Auschwitz.

SARI FRIEDMAN's poems and stories have appeared in *The Manhattan Poetry Review, Stroker,* and other publications. She teaches technical and creative writing classes at the New York Institute of Technology. Her father and grandfather were incarcerated during the Holocaust, and some of her relatives were murdered.

JOSEPH GLAZER's poetry has been widely published in the United States. He came to America from Russo-Poland at the age of eight. He lost a large extended family there—grandparents, uncles, aunts, cousins. Only one cousin survived his Buchenwald experiences and lives in Atlanta. "My earliest recollection of the dread oncoming fate was before WWII. I was very young and was saving stamps at the time. My mother had just received a postcard from her sister stating everything was just fine, normal. I peeled off the stamp and read the message underneath: 'Mir shtarbn fun hoonger' (we're dying of hunger.)"

BARBARA GOLDBERG's poetry has appeared in *Poetry,* the *American Scholar, NER/BLQ,* and other publications. She has also published a book, *Berta Broadfoot and Pepin the Short: A Merovingian Romance.* She was the only member of her family born in the United States. Her father was born in Germany and her mother in Czechoslovakia. They fled Prague in 1938 and lived in Paris until the Nazis invaded France; then they fled to Portugal, Brazil, and entered the United States on a Brazilian visa. Several members of her family were in the camps; her maternal grandmother perished in transport to one of the camps in 1943.

ANNETTE BIALIK HARCHIK's poetry has been widely published in anthologies, small press magazines, and newspapers. She is the poetry editor of *Response* magazine and a cofounder of the Poetry Kibbutz. Both of her parents are the sole survivors of their large families from Poland. Her mother was in the Lodz ghetto, Auschwitz, and Dachau. Her father was in the Posnan Lager, Auschwitz, and Dachau. Harchik was born in Belgium, where her parents settled after they met and married, right after Dachau was liberated. The family emigrated to the United States in 1951.

WILLIAM HEYEN, an American and the son of a German of the generation which produced the Nazis, "feels that he must confront the Nazi murder of the Jews, and discover both how far he is attached to his heritage and how far he must repudiate it" (Richard Wilbur). His poetry and prose have been widely published. Heyen's books include *Erika—Poems of the Holocaust, The Swastika Poems, The City Parables,* and many others. He is a professor of English at the State University of New York, Brockport.

BARBARA HELFGOTT HYETT teaches writing at Boston University. Her book, *In Evidence: Poems of the Liberation of Nazi Concentration Camps,* was published by the University of Pittsburgh Press in 1986. Her work has also appeared in the *New Republic,* the *Nation,* and *Ploughshares.* Her father was a veteran of World War II, and she had the opportunity to interview GIs who liberated the Nazi camps. Many members of her family were killed in the camps.

PHYLLIS KAHANEY teaches English at the University of San Diego; her poetry and translations have been widely published. Her grandparents are Russian and escaped the Holocaust; her two great-aunts, however, were killed along with their husbands at Babi Yar.

SHARON KESSLER lives in Jerusalem and teaches English as a second language at Hebrew University. Her poetry has appeared in various journals in Israel and the United States. Her maternal grandparents immigrated to the United States from Warsaw in the 1920s; the rest of the family remained behind and it is unknown what became of them.

DENYSE KIRSCH is a writer who lives in Israel. Her father left his village of Radviliskis in Lithuania during the 1930s and fled to South Africa. His parents and sister were wiped out with the other Jews in the area. "In July 1941, the Lithuanian army rounded up all the Jews, assembled them in the synagogue in Birzai on the Latvian border, and then marched them out to the nearby forests, where they first had to dig their own mass grave."

DAVID LAMPERT is the author of *The Wind in the Fire,* a book of poetry, and his poems have appeared in several issues of the *Berkeley Poets Cooperative.* His paternal ancestors were German, and although most of them left Germany prior to the Holocaust, it has been an influence on his life and poetry.

STEVEN C. LEVI is a free-lance writer and part-time college instructor who lives in Alaska. He has eight books in print and is currently working on his eighth novel. His father's grandparents were deported from Torino, Italy, in 1940. The grandfather died in a work camp (at the age of 93) and the grandmother perished in Auschwitz. Levi's father and family fled to Paris in 1939, and then escaped from France to the United States eighteen months later.

LYN LIFSHIN is an internationally known poet and editor. More than seventy of her books and chapbooks have been published, and she has edited a series of books of women's writing. Her poems have appeared in various major literary magazines in the United States. Many of her relatives were killed in the Holocaust.

RACHEL LODEN's poems have appeared in a number of magazines and anthologies. Members of her family perished in mass shootings near Kiev, in the Ukraine, in 1941.

SEYMOUR MAYNE is a professor of English at the University of Ottawa in Canada. His poetry has been widely published; his books include *The Impossible Promised Land, Vanguard of Dreams, Children of Abel,* and others. His mother was the last person in her family to leave the Bialystok area of Poland successfully; the others perished.

RICHARD MICHELSON is a poet who lives in Amherst, Massachusetts. His books include *Tap Dancing for the Relatives* (University Presses of Florida, 1985) and *The Head of the Family* (Red Herring Press, 1978.)

CHRISTOPHER MILLIS recently lived in Italy on a Fulbright Grant to translate the work of the Jewish poet Umberto Saba. Millis's work has appeared in journals in the United States and in Europe. His play, "The Magnetic Properties of Moonlight," was produced off Broadway in 1984.

MARK NEPO's poetry has been widely published in such journals as *Antaeus, Southern Review,* and *Kenyon Review.* He also has two books of poetry, *God, The Maker of the Bed, and The Painter* and *Fire Without Witness.* Seven members of his family died in the Holocaust. His aunt Rifkah, the subject of his poem in this book, was sent steamship tickets to America by her brother in New York in 1933; she sent them back, unused, claiming that Budapest was her home. She and her family were not heard from after 1939.

AMOS NEUFELD is a widely published poet and is an editor of a weekly New York City Jewish newspaper. He is an Israeli-born son of Holocaust survivors. His parents are from Czechoslavakia; his father was in slave labor camps from 1939 to 1944, and his mother and her family were sent to Auschwitz in 1944. After the war, his parents married and lived in Budapest for two years, then in Prague for two years, then lived in Israel for nine years before coming to New York.

GAIL NEWMAN is a poet and San Francisco coordinator of California Poets in the Schools. She was born in Lansberg, Germany, in 1946. Her parents are both Polish Jews; her mother was born in Lodz and spent time in the Lodz ghetto and in Auschwitz, and her father, born in Bzeziny, spent time in the Bzeziny ghetto, the Lodz ghetto, Auschwitz, and Dachau. Her mother is the sole survivor of an extended family of over three hundred. Newman and her family moved to America in 1948.

GARY PACERNICK's poems have appeared in various journals including the *American Poetry Review* and *Poetry Now*. He has also published a book, *The Jewish Poems* (Wright State University Press, 1985.) His father is from the Ukraine and his mother's family is from Poland; many relatives from both sides of the family were killed during the Holocaust.

EVELYN POSAMENTIER has written several books of poetry, and her work has been published in various magazines including the *American Poetry Review*. Her parents are from Vienna and fled to England in 1939; they arrived in New York City in 1940. Her four grandparents were killed in concentration camps. This publication of her poems is dedicated to the memory of her parents, Ernest and Alice Posamentier, and her grandparents, Otto and Gisela Epstein Pisk and Heinrich and Ernestine Schick Posamentier.

KAREN PROPP's poems have appeared in *Ploughshares*, the *Agni Review*, and *Ironwood*. She received a Ph.D. in writing from the University of Utah and is currently living in the Boston area. Her mother's family fled Vienna in 1937, lived in hiding in Brussels, and emigrated to the Bronx on the last boat to leave Europe in 1939.

ANNE RANASINGHE's poems, stories, and radio plays have been published in Sri Lanka and abroad in journals and anthologies. She was born in Germany and fled to England just prior to World War II. She was the only one from her immediate family who survived the Holocaust. She now lives in Colombo, Sri Lanka, with her husband and children.

LISA RESS's book *Flight Patterns* was the 1983 winner of the Associated Writing Programs' Award Series in Poetry, and was published by the University Press of Virginia in 1985. She is currently assistant professor of English at Hollins College in Roanoke, Virginia. She was born of Viennese parents in Tangier, Morocco, in 1939. Most of her father's relatives fled Europe in time, though some were killed. Most of her mother's family was not quite as fortunate; her mother's parents were killed at Auschwitz. Ress and her parents came to the United States in 1941 and settled in Chicago.

IRENE RETI lives in Santa Cruz, California, where she runs a lesbian-feminist press, HerBooks. Her father was born in Budapest and spent the war years in Turkey; her mother is from Germany.

ELIZABETH ROSNER is a writer, instructor, and editor in Berkeley, California. Her father, born in Hamburg, was deported to Buchenwald in 1944 and remained there until liberation in 1945. Her mother, born in Vilna, managed to escape from the Vilna ghetto just before it was liquidated, and remained in hiding until the Russians arrived. Both of their surviving families found refuge in Sweden after the war; her parents met there, married in Israel, and came to the United States in 1951.

JANE SCHAPIRO's poems have appeared in various magazines including *Moment* and *Poetry East*. Many members of her family lived in Europe during the Holocaust.

DAVID SHEVIN is assistant professor of English at Tiffin University in Ohio. He has published essays, poetry, reportage, and translations. His books include *What Happens* (1983) and *The Stop Book* (1978). Most of his family came from Lithuania and settled in upstate New York between 1910 and 1920. The family that remained in Europe mostly perished in the Holocaust.

NANCY SHIFFRIN writes poetry, reviews, and nonfiction in Los Angeles. Her poetry has appeared in various journals including the *New York Quarterly* and *Amelia*. Many members of her family lived in Europe during the Holocaust; some of them escaped from concentration camps.

ENID SHOMER's poems and stories have appeared in *Poetry*, *Ploughshares*, and many other magazines and anthologies. She is the author

185

of *Stalking the Florida Panther* (Word Works, 1987), a collection of poems. Her husband is the only child from the town of Kremenets in the Volhynia who survived the Holocaust.

BARRY STERNLIEB's poetry has appeared in various journals including *Poetry* and *Prairie Schooner*. His first book, *Fission* (Adastra Press), was published in 1986. His grandfather and his family moved to America from Poland in the early 1900s. His uncle and aunt remained in Europe and died in Auschwitz.

MARIE SYRKIN is a well-known author, lecturer, editor, and teacher. Her poetry and nonfiction have been widely published. She has written several books, including the authoritative biography *Golda Meir— Israel's Leader*. She is on the editorial board of *Midstream*, a Zionist monthly. Most of her mother's family—twenty-one men, women, and children—were murdered by the Nazis in Poland and Latvia.

ALINA TUGEND is a journalist who is a native of Los Angeles, California. Her grandmother served as president of the Women's International Zionist Organization in Germany from 1936 to 1939. In that capacity, she led two groups of Jewish children from Germany to New York, in 1937 and 1938. In 1939, she and her family left Berlin to resettle in America.

MORRIE WARSHAWSKI is a free-lance writer and arts consultant living in San Francisco. His work has been published in various journals including the *New York Quarterly* and *Mississippi Mud*. He was born in Badnauheim, Germany, just after the war. His parents are from Poland; both of them were in a number of camps and ended the war in Auschwitz and Bergen-Belsen.

DORA WEEKS was a poet and attorney who lived in California. Her father was born in Poland and her mother, in Rumania.

FLORENCE WEINBERGER's poetry has been published in numerous journals including *Lilith* and *Nimrod*. Her first book of poems *The Invisible Telling Its Shape*, was published in 1988. Her parents immigrated from Hungary to New York in 1923 and 1930; she lost many aunts, uncles, and cousins in the Holocaust. Her husband, also from Hungary, is a survivor.

WILL WELLS's poetry has been published in various journals including the *Southern Poetry Review*. His book, *Conversing with the Light* (Anhinga Press, 1988), was selected for the 1987 Anhinga Award. He teaches English and creative writing at Lima Technical College and Ohio State University in Lima, Ohio. His mother lived on a small vineyard near Thionville in Lorraine (France) before she became a displaced person because of the strategic location of the property. His father was an American GI.

EVELYN WEXLER's poems have appeared in several literary journals including *Croton Review* and the *Philadelphia Poets*. She moved from New York to Budapest with her mother in 1936 at the age of eleven to join her uncle, a lawyer, because he could afford to pay for medical treatment her mother needed. In 1937, her father wrote from America urging the entire family to flee, to avoid the catastrophe predicted by the American press. She and her mother left; most of the others perished at Auschwitz and Dachau.

C. K. WILLIAMS has published many books of poetry including *Lies* (1969), *I Am the Bitter Name* (1972), *With Ignorance* (1977), and *Tar* (1983). His latest book of poetry is *Flesh and Blood*, published in 1987 by Farrar, Straus and Giroux. He is a professor of English at George Mason University and is currently living in Paris. Some of his relatives lived in Europe during the Holocaust and did not survive.

MERRA YOUNG-PROTTENGEIER is a psychotherapist in private practice in Minneapolis, Minnesota. She is a member of the Women Poets of the Twin Cities. Her father grew up in a small town in Lithuania and spent time in Birkinau and Auschwitz.

Acknowledgments

Marvin Bell's "The Extermination of the Jews" first appeared in Marvin Bell, *A Probable Volume of Dreams* (Atheneum, 1969); "Getting Lost in Nazi Germany" first appeared in Marvin Bell, *The Escape into You* (Atheneum, 1971). Reprinted by permission.

Talia N. Bloch's "While Bouncing the Shema Back and Forth in Shul" first appeared in *Achshav* 31, no. 4 (Summer 1982).

BonniLee's "White Candles" first appeared in *Conceptions Southwest* 10: no. 2.

Susan Dambroff's "Resistance" first appeared in Susan Dambroff, *Memory in Bone* (Black Oyster Press, 1984).

Joan (Thaler) Dobbie's "Forty Three Years After Hitler My Parents Visit Eugene" first appeared in Joan Dobbie, *A Trip through Mama Kali's Zoological Garden*, 1984.

Stewart J. Florsheim's "Weekend in Palm Springs" first appeared in *J.A.C.O.B.'s Letter* 6, no. 2 (Spring 1986): 6; "The Jewish Singles Event" first appeared in *The Round Table* 3, no. 1 (Spring 1986): 8.

Barbara Goldberg's "Our Father" first appeared in *Folio* 2, no. 2 (Fall 1985): 36.

Annette Bialik Harchik's "Requiem" first appeared in *Response* 48 (Spring 1985).

William Heyen's "Blue," "The Trains," "For Hermann Heyen," "The Numinous," and "To the Onlookers" reprinted from *Erika: Poems of the Holocaust* by William Heyen by permission of the publisher, Vanguard Press, Inc. Copyright © 1977 & 1984 by William Heyen.

Phyllis Kahaney's "Pogrom" first appeared in *Eye Prayers* (Tuolumne Press, 1981); "Germany, 1981" first appeared in *The Wooster Review* 5 (Spring 1986).

Sharon Kessler's "Family Secrets" and "Names the Dead Speak" first appeared in *Seven Gates* (Summer 1985).

Rachel Loden's "Conversations with Dr. M" first appeared in *Kalliope* 9, no. 3 (1987): 8–9.

Seymour Mayne's "In Memory of Aaron, Murdered Grandfather" first appeared in *Children of Abel* (Mosaic Press, 1986); "Zalman" first appeared in *The Impossible Promised Land: Poems New and Selected* (Mosaic Press, 1981).

Richard Michelson's "Interrogation" first appeared in *Nimrod*, Awards VII issue (1985); "The Jews That We Are" first appeared in Richard Michelson, *Tap Dancing for the Relatives* (University Presses of Florida, 1985); "Where I Sat" first appeared in *Jewish Currents* (May, 1982); "Genuine Jewish Flesh" first appeared in *Bellingham Review* (Fall 1984).

Amos Neufeld's "Pictures and Stories" first appeared in *Martyrdom and Resistance* (November–December, 1984); "Children of Night" first appeared in *Genesis 2* (December–January, 1984–85); "Family Album" first appeared in *Jewish Frontier* (March–April, 1987).

Acknowledgments

Gail Newman's "An Anti-Semitic Demonstration" first appeared in Eva Poole-Gilson et al., eds., *Thread Winding in the Loom of Eternity: California Poets in the Schools Statewide Anthology, 1987* (California Poets in the Schools, 1987).

Evelyn Posamentier's "Counting Backwards" first appeared in the *American Poetry Review* 7, no. 3 (1978).

Anne Ranasinghe's "Auschwitz from Columbo" first appeared in *Present Tense* 2, no. 3 (Spring 1975): 53; "Holocaust 1944" first appeared in the *Jerusalem Post*, Copyright *Jerusalem Post*.

Lisa Ress' "The Family Album," "Waving Her Farewell," "Household Rules," "Learning the Ropes" and "The Visit" first appeared in Lisa Ress, *Flight Patterns* (University Press of Virginia, 1985). Reprinted by permission.

Irene Reti's "I Never Knew I Was Jewish" first appeared in Sue McCabe, Irene Reti, and Terese Armstrong, eds., *Lesbian Words: Photographs and Writings* (HerBooks, 1985).

Jane Schapiro's "The Tourist" first appeared in *Black Bear Review* 4 (Spring 1986).

Nancy Shiffrin's "Anna's Dream" first appeared in Nancy Shiffrin, *What She Could Not Name* (La Jolla Poets Press, 1987).

Enid Shomer's "Women Bathing at Bergen-Belsen" first appeared in *Negative Capability* 6, no. 1 (Winter 1986).

Marie Syrkin's "My Uncle in Treblinka" first appeared in Marie Syrkin, *Gleanings: Selected Verse* (Rhythms Press, 1979).

Florence Weinberger's "Survivor" first appeared in *Poetry/LA*, no. 11 (Fall–Winter 1985–86).

Will Wells's "Beatings" first appeared in *Southern Poetry Review* 25, no. 1 (Spring 1985): 27.

Index of Poets

Alkalay-Gut, Karen, 47

Bell, Marvin, 129, 130
Berg, Stephen, 23
Bloch, Talia N., 159
BonniLee, 73

Dambroff, Susan, 161
Dobbie, Joan (Thaler), 95

Fish, Cheryl J., 76
Fishman, Charles, 165
Florsheim, Stewart J., 30, 78, 97, 99
Freed, Florence Wallach, 102
Friedman, Sari, 103, 104

Glazer, Joseph, 131
Goldberg, Barbara, 80, 107

Harchik, Annette Bialik, 48, 82
Heyen, William, 32, 34, 50, 133, 166
Hyett, Barbara Helfgott, 35

Kahaney, Phyllis, 51, 167
Kessler, Sharon, 52, 53
Kirsch, Denyse, 54

Lampert, David, 135
Levi, Steven C., 55
Lifshin, Lyn, 36, 38, 39, 83, 137
Loden, Rachel, 170

Mayne, Seymour, 57, 172
Michelson, Richard, 40, 41, 108, 110,
    112, 173

Millis, Christopher, 138

Nepo, Mark, 58
Neufeld, Amos, 59, 60, 175
Newman, Gail, 84, 114, 139

Pacernick, Gary, 85
Posamentier, Evelyn, 61, 63, 115, 116
Propp, Karen, 140

Ranasinghe, Anne, 42, 142, 144
Ress, Lisa, 65, 86, 118, 146, 147
Reti, Irene, 119
Rosner, Elizabeth, 87

Schapiro, Jane, 124
Shevin, David, 148
Shiffrin, Nancy, 150
Shomer, Enid, 44
Sternlieb, Barry, 88
Syrkin, Marie, 66

Tugend, Alina, 151

Warshawski, Morrie, 89
Weeks, Dora, 125
Weinberger, Florence, 90, 91
Wells, Will, 92
Wexler, Evelyn, 67
Williams, C. K., 152, 176

Young-Prottengeier, Merra, 69

Stewart J. Florsheim lives in San Francisco and manages a technical publications department for a computer software company. His poetry has appeared in small press publications including *Berkeley Poets Cooperative, The Round Table, Blue Unicorn, Syracuse Poems,* and *Men Talk,* an anthology of male experience poetry. His translations of Sarah Kirsch and Burghild Holzer have been published in *Dimension* (University of Texas, Austin). Mr. Florsheim's parents are from Germany: his mother came to the United States in 1939 and his father in 1934.

The manuscript was prepared for publication by Christina Postema. The book was designed by Joanne Kinney. The typeface for the text and the display is Palatino. The book is printed on 55-lb. Glatfelter text paper and is bound in Arrestox linen.

Manufactured in the United States of America.